D0563266

Cranmer's Church

Cranmer's Church

Introducing the Episcopal Church and Anglicanism in America

Chuck Collins

THE
WATERCRESS
PRESS

San Antonio
2005

Copyright © 2005 by Chuck Collins
All rights reserved

A Watercress Press book
from *Geron & Associates*

Cover design by Ellen Collins
Cover photo by Ansen Seale
Book design by Fishead Productions

For additional copies:
Christ Church
510 Belknap
San Antonio, TX 78212

ISBN 978-0-934955-62-1
Library of Congress Catalog Card Number 2005935891

Introduction

Thomas Cranmer is my reluctant hero. There were good reasons to title this book something else: *Wycliff's Church, Richard Hooker's Church, Queen Elizabeth's Church,* or *C. S. Lewis' Church.* There was also reason to not name this after any one person because, unlike Lutherans and Presbyterians, this church does not rally around the personality and thoughts of a single individual. But Cranmer was the first Archbishop of Canterbury in the newly formed Church of England and a leading architect of Anglicanism. He didn't particularly want the job, was ill equipped for the responsibilities, and was not an intellectual or charismatic giant like the great reformers. His greatest gift was as an organizer rather than an original thinker.[1] But as its spokesman, Cranmer gradually helped steer the Church of England through rough waters into Protestantism. By authoring the first two Prayer Books and the Articles of Religion he defined the character of theology and worship in the Church of England. Someone called him the "Teflon Prelate"[2] because he was sometimes illusive and his ideas were always evolving. But at the end, he paid with his life for his belief in the supremacy of Holy Scripture, and the doctrines of "Justification by Faith" and the "Priesthood of all Believers." He is remembered here for his courage to question the hallowed traditions of his day and follow the leading of his reformed heart.

The chapters of this book were written over the twenty-five years I've been a priest. They were written to address issues about our history, the theological underpinnings of Episcopalianism, and more practical matters of why we worship the way we do and what membership means. I wrote this specifically to instruct new members to the Episcopal Church about our distinctives and to help older members who have forgotten the strength of our heritage. There is also in these chapters more than a hint of wanting to defend what is being challenged in our day by those who don't seem to care much about our history or our corporate Anglican identity. In some ways this is the worst possible time to write about the

1   See Notes beginning on page 93.

Episcopal Church because only God knows what will remain after the current realignment. For decades we have neglected our foundations. I admit that I am not very hopeful about our future as a denomination, but I am very hopeful that out of the ashes will come a church that is faithful again to historic Anglicanism — that is the subject of this book.

I am grateful for the people of St. Mark's on the Mesa Episcopal Church (Albuquerque, NM) for their support and friendship over many years. Thanks especially for giving me sabbatical time away to begin this project and for teaching me how to teach. And I thank my current church family, Christ Episcopal Church (San Antonio, TX), for standing with me for the things that really matter in our struggle for the heart and soul of the Episcopal Church.

I dedicate this to all who are unafraid to examine their faith, especially to my children: Noel, Alison, Hope, and Andrew. This comes with my prayers for you and anyone who might pick this up, even if it's the only thing to read in a laundromat, required reading for a new members class, or punishment for acting up in youth group. I am grateful for the constant encouragement of my wife, Ellen, and the kind encouragement and advice of The Very Rev. Dr. Paul Zahl, The Rev. Dr. Les Fairfield, The Rev. Dr. Frank Williams, and a number of friends who did the painful work of reading the first drafts to give me much valuable feedback.

Years ago I vowed to not pay attention to authors who have the annoying habit of making simple and obvious things complicated. My goal is just the opposite; I want to make the matters of the faith as reachable and understandable as they really are. To the extent that I have succeeded, TO GOD BE THE GLORY!

Pages cited are from *The Book of Common Prayer* (1979), and Bible verses are from *The New Revised Standard Version*.

Contents

Chapter 1

How can I join a church started by a líbido?

Okay, so admit it: the popular idea that King Henry VIII started the Church of England, the mother church of the Episcopal Church, is a little embarrassing. This is the same "Henry" who enjoyed six different wives and had a few killed along the way! Sure, this sixteenth-century monarch was desperate for a male heir to the throne, and, sure, he wanted a divorce so that he could marry beautiful Anne Boleyn.[3] But who wants the genesis of their denomination hinging on the runaway libido of a desperate king of England? The facts of history save us the embarrassment. The Episcopal Church did not start with Henry. We have a much earlier and nobler beginning.

The Church of England goes all the way back to Jesus Christ and the apostles. In the Creed Episcopalians recite every Sunday we affirm our belief in the "catholic and apostolic" church. This means that we hold to Jesus and to the teaching of the apostles — as our founder and foundations. We are *catholic* (not "Roman Catholic") in the sense that we subscribe to the teaching of the church that is true for all people at all times (i.e., "universal").[4] And we are *apostolic* because we believe that the Episcopal Church has its origins and authority in the enduring truth of the apostolic teaching recorded in Holy Scripture.

No one knows for sure when Christianity first came to Britain. There's a far-fetched tradition that Joseph of Arimathaea (of biblical fame,

1

Matthew 27:57) brought Christianity to the island, along with the Holy Grail, the supposed cup of the Last Supper. It's more likely that traders or Roman soldiers first introduced Christianity in the second and third centuries. Britain's first Christian martyr, St. Alban, was killed there in the third century. And three English bishops attended the Synod of Arles — France (A.D. 314), suggesting that the church in England was well organized by that date.

The most ancient form of Christianity in Britain was not Roman Catholicism, as many people assume, but "Celtic" Christianity. The Celts were not originally a Boston basketball team or a style of jewelry; rather, they were a loose association of Christians who subscribed to a simple austere expression of Christianity. They were organized around monasteries with abbots instead of dioceses with bishops. It was an expression that highly valued nature, hermits, and monks. But because of the influence of such missionaries as Augustine, the Benedictine monk sent by the pope in A.D. 597, Britain gradually turned toward Rome. At the Synod of Whitby (A.D. 664) the English Church formally decided to follow the practices of the Latin church over the Celts. But even with the new allegiance to Rome, British monarchs retained the right to approve all church appointments.

As the church moved into the Middle Ages, it evolved into something very different from the way it began. "Tradition" gradually began to assume a separate but equal status as an authority alongside the Bible. This opened the door for all kinds of unbiblical and extra-biblical practices and beliefs. This included: mandatory celibacy for clergy, purgatory (the idea that there is a state of temporary punishment after death), and the practice of praying to the saints. Increasingly, salvation was considered something that could be earned by doing certain religious acts instead of God's gracious love and free gift. Holy Communion became an elaborate re-sacrifice on an altar in which bread and wine were thought to become the actual body and blood of Jesus Christ. What was originally meant to be "mystery" surrounding the Sunday services acquired a more "magical" quality (the term "hocus pocus" is derived from the Latin phrase for "This is my body"). The liturgy was recited in Latin and was barely understood by the clergy, much less by the average churchgoers. Added to the growing undercurrent of discontent was the terrible moral and educational decline of many of the clergy. It was not uncommon for priests to have mistresses, to be in the ministry for their own financial gain, and to be absent from their churches for long periods of time.

John Wycliff (1320-1384) was "England's first true Protestant."[5] By the time he arrived on the scene the pump was primed for the century-long reformation of the church that followed in his wake. Wycliff was the leading theologian and philosopher of Europe's most outstanding university, the University of Oxford. His aim, and the aim of all the English reformers, was to reinstate Holy Scripture as the primary authority for the church. This posed a clear and present challenge to the treasured doctrines of the medieval Catholic Church. Adding fuel to the reforming fires were the writings of Martin Luther in Germany that were illegally finding their way into England. Especially affected by Luther's inflammatory ideas was a group of English academics at Cambridge University (that included Cranmer and Tyndale, mentioned later). The White Horse Tavern in Cambridge became the hangout for those interested in discussing the Bible and the German reformers. These religious stirrings, the invention of the moveable type printing press (1450), the translation of the Bible into English (1526), and the rise of humanism (encouraging the study of Hebrew and Greek) all paved the way for a major Reformation of the church in England.

At the same time that momentum for religious reformation was gaining, steam was also building on the political front. Henry VIII was looking for a political solution to dissolve his inconvenient marriage to Catherine of Aragon. He frantically wanted to father a male heir to the throne. In 1534, when the pope refused to act on his behalf, Henry took the advice of his new Archbishop of Canterbury, Thomas Cranmer, and declared that the Bishop of Rome had no authority over English bishops. By an act of Parliament, Henry was named the "supreme head" of the Church of

England. After centuries of labor pains, political and theological, the Church of England was born! Henry remained Roman Catholic in his practices until he died, but by starting an independent branch of the Catholic Church he made a way for the religious and theological Reformation in England. Although he never embraced Protestantism as such, he opened the door for the reformation by legalizing the English Bible, abolishing monasticism in Britain, and having his son, the future King Edward VI, educated by Protestants. It's significant that, on his deathbed, instead of asking for sacramental Last Rites, Henry reportedly came to a personal faith in Christ.[6]

Our official title is "The Protestant Episcopal Church." This links us permanently to the Protestant principles of the English Reformation: the Bible as supreme authority (over tradition, reason, and experience),[7] "Justification by Faith" alone (we can be right with God by receiving in faith what Jesus accomplished for us on the cross, not by being 'religious' or 'good'), and the "Priesthood of all Believers" (we don't need a priest or any other intermediary to relate to God personally).

Edward VI, Henry's son, ascended to the throne in 1547. Under Edward, the Protestant rumblings of the previous 200 years finally coalesced. The boy King was nine years old when he was crowned and he ruled only six years before his untimely death. But enormous changes took place during those years. The Mass, formerly in Latin, was written in common English. Communion tables replaced altars, and wine, previously reserved for clergy only, was distributed along with the bread to all communicants. Clergy were also permitted to marry under Edward's reign. After he died the Church of England experienced a five-year reversion back to Catholicism under Queen Mary. She was called "Bloody Mary" because she ordered killed a number of prominent Protestant leaders. On her hit list was Archbishop Cranmer who was burned at the stake March 21, 1556. A month earlier, in a weak moment, Cranmer was persuaded to sign three recantations of his Protestant views. But, "of all the martyrs, strange to say, none at the last moment showed more physical courage than Cranmer did."[8] As the fire was burning around him he reportedly put his hand into the flames and said, "this unworthy right hand," referring to his previous recantation. He died bravely for the cause of the Protestant Reformation in England.

When Mary died, Elizabeth returned the church to Protestantism and brought a certain settlement to "Anglican"[9] theology and worship, albeit a somewhat watered-down compromise that made no one happy in the end.[10] During her 45-year reign as queen (1558–1603), Elizabeth sought a balance upholding the church's Scripture basis (i.e., Protestant) while not totally abandoning the richness of Catholicism. Unlike other Protestant churches born at the same time, a conscious decision was made to retain certain institutions (like bishops) and ceremonies of the western Catholic Church that did not conflict with the teaching of Holy Scripture.

In our history there has obviously not been full agreement about all matters of theology and piety. The parties present at the Reformation — Catholics, Reformers and Humanists — and their offspring, have kept the dialogue alive and interesting. And the mantle of leadership of the Episcopal Church has gone back and forth between these groups. But while there is plenty of room for debate about secondary issues, there has been substantial agreement over the years about a fixed doctrinal core. The English Reformation, church councils, and the various formularies have consistently affirmed certain defining principles. Namely: the primary authority for Anglicans (the Church of England and the Episcopal Church) is the Bible, and the Bible's central teachings are preserved in the creeds and in the prayers of our liturgy (the Prayer Book).

This is a heritage to be proud of. Many Episcopal laypersons and clergy have forever affected church and society. One literally gave his life to see the Bible translated into English — William Tyndale. Another wrote the first two versions of the Book of Common Prayer (1549 and 1552), enshrining the essentials of our Episcopal faith in the context of our worship — Thomas Cranmer. One wrote over 5,000 hymns, including "Hark! The Herald Angels Sing" — Charles Wesley. As a member of

Parliament, another Anglican led the movement that resulted in the abolition of slavery in England – William Wilberforce. It was an Anglican who wrote one of the most effective instruments to bring people to faith in Jesus Christ in modern times, *Mere Christianity* by C. S. Lewis. As Archbishop in South Africa, another led the fight against apartheid in his country and injustices around the world – Desmond Tutu. More presidents of the U.S. have been Episcopalian than any other denomination, and courageous Anglicans around the world are known for upholding the biblical faith and as crusaders for the dignity of every human being.

DISCUSSION QUESTIONS

1. Did Henry VIII start the Episcopal Church?

2. How is the church "catholic" and "apostolic?"
    (Nicene Creed p. 328; see also p. 854)

3. What is the most ancient expression of Christianity in England?
    Why is this significant?

4. Is the Episcopal Church "Protestant" or "Catholic"?

5. Read Rom. 3:21-26 and Eph. 2:8-9. Discuss the difference between
    Justification by Faith and Justification by Works. (Justification simply
    means "being made right with God.")

6. If you are a new Episcopalian, what is it that originally drew you to
    the Episcopal Church? If you are a life-long Episcopalian, what keeps
    you coming?

Chapter 2

Anglicans arrive in America

It's possible to visit an Episcopal church today that transports you back to the Middle Ages: where incense is burned, elaborate clergy vestments are worn, and the Bible readings are chanted. And just down the street is another Episcopal church where few or no formal vestments are worn, guitars have replaced the organ, and the minister is virtually indistinguishable from an enthusiastic Baptist preacher. There are all kinds of Episcopal churches: high and low, evangelistic and social action, traditional and charismatic. The differences are largely explained by how the Church of England was introduced to America, and by the dialogue between the different streams of thought (described as "parties") that make up the Episcopal Church.

Here's how it started. Although there were occasional Church of England services in America before 1600, the official birthday of the Episcopal Church is generally agreed to be June 16, 1607. This is the day Captain John Smith and 104 others celebrated the Lord's Supper with their Church of England priest-chaplain, Robert Hunt, commemorating their safe arrival to Jamestown, Virginia. Jamestown was the first permanent English colony in America. The expression of faith they brought with them was that of the 16th century Protestant Reformation.[11]

The word "Episcopal" is the English equivalent of the Greek word for "bishop." With such an emphasis you might think that bishops played an important role in the early years of Anglicanism in America. Surprisingly, they were not in the picture at all! For almost two hundred years the Episcopal Church did not have a resident bishop to perform confirmations, ordain clergy, consecrate new churches, or form hierarchical diocesan structures. *The Book of Common Prayer* was the glue that kept the church together during its formative years. Many Puritans, some of them Anglicans, were perfectly happy with this arrangement because they believed that bishops from the Church of England would try to sway politics in England's favor in the colonies.

Between 1730 and 1745 the evangelical revival that began in England spilled over into America. "The Great Awakening," as it was called, was closely associated with Church of England evangelists. George Whitefield in America and his counterpart in England, John Wesley, both attracted huge crowds who were hungry for a personal relationship with the living Lord. Wesley started what was at first sarcastically called "Methodism." This renewal movement inside the Church of England taught the importance of personal faith for appropriating God's grace. Wesley remained an Anglican priest all his life, but soon after he died Methodist proponents left to form their own denomination. Regrettably, most members of the Church of England ignored Whitefield, Wesley, and the 18th century revival, opposing the "religious enthusiasm" that often accompanied their ministry.

England's Church in America at the time of the American Revolution was holding on by the smallest thread. As the Revolutionary War heated up, many clergy returned to England because they had sworn allegiance to the crown. The Declaration of Independence (1776) signified many changes, among which was the inevitable break of the American Church of England into the first independent branch of Anglicanism.[12] They changed the name in 1785 for obvious reasons from The Church of England to "The Protestant Episcopal Church in the United States of America."[13] Even though it took some time to iron out the details for a new form of governance, the main concern for the first Episcopalians "was to insure the continued existence of the faith, order, and worship of the Anglican Communion in the United States of America."[14]

Two strong personalities dominated the early years of the Episcopal Church: Samuel Seabury and William White. These men represented two very different philosophies that competed to determine the character of the Episcopal Church. Seabury was sent by Connecticut clergymen to England to seek consecration (ordination to be bishop). After an unsuccessful year of pleading with English authorities, in 1784 he went to Scotland where he was consecrated the first bishop of the Episcopal Church.[15] As part of the agreement he made to be consecrated, Seabury agreed to introduce certain elements of the Scottish Prayer Book into the Episcopal Church. In the meantime, White was the rector of Christ Church in Philadelphia. At the urging of the Archbishop of Canterbury, White dismissed Seabury's consecration as invalid. The result was two rival Episcopal churches in the United States, one led by Seabury with an "irregular" consecration and the other by White who was not yet a bishop. White was finally consecrated "properly" in England in 1787.

Seabury and White strongly disagreed with one another about how to configure the new church. Seabury wanted a bishop-dominated structure like the English model while White argued for much greater priest and lay involvement based on the representative democratic model of the American political system. Seabury saw the diocese as the most important unit of government while White thought that bishops and dioceses exist only to support the parishes.[16] After significant debate, and for the sake of unity, Seabury conceded to White's proposals for an American Prayer Book, and both factions were brought together for the General Convention of 1789. It was mostly White's ideas that shaped the Episcopal denominational structure. He fought for and won the adoption of the Thirty-Nine Articles as the theological standard for the American Church (see p. 867). White also published a reading list that influenced several generations of priests ordained in the Episcopal Church.

Even though there has been a settled agreement throughout the history of the Episcopal Church about its core values, including the authority of Scripture,[17] differences in theological perspectives and worship styles are attributable to the ongoing dialogue (and sometimes outright wrestling match!) between three major theological parties: evangelical, high church, and rationalists.

EVANGELICALS take their bearings from the 16th century Protestant Reformation and the English reformers took their bearing from the Bible and the early church fathers. They came into their own as a "party" in the 1830's.[18] Evangelicals, generally speaking, believe in the five "*solas*" of the Reformation: *Scriptura, Christo, Gratia, Fide, and Soli Deo Gloria.* They believe that the Bible is the ultimate authority; that Jesus Christ is the sole mediator between God and humankind and the only way to salvation; that salvation is a free gift of God for those who are too sinful and "fallen" to deserve it; that entrance into God's kingdom is by believing and receiving the benefits of the cross of Christ; and that life is not to be divided into "sacred and secular," but rather every aspect of our lives is to be lived for God and his glory.

There are a significant number of evangelicals in the Episcopal Church today, and of the more than 80 million Anglicans in the world, by far the vast majority of them (mostly in Africa and Asia) are evangelicals. At least three times in our history certain evangelicals left to start their own churches: after John Wesley died many of his followers left the Church of England to form the Methodist Church; in 1873 a small group of evangelicals, led by the Assistant Bishop of Kentucky, George David Cummins, broke away to start the Reformed Episcopal Church; and in 2000 a group of Episcopalians led by two newly consecrated bishops, Chuck Murphy and John Rogers, left the Episcopal Church to start the Anglican Mission in America as an extension of the Provinces of Rwanda and Southeast Asia.

The *HIGH CHURCH* party takes its cue from pre-Reformation Catholic ideals. Whereas evangelicals saw the Bible as the primary authority, High Churchmen tended to believe in "Scripture plus" certain other sources of authority. They value tradition and the councils of the church as an equal authority to the Bible. In 1833 a group of scholars at Oxford University began publishing a series of religious tracts. The Tractarians, as they were called, sought to interpret Scripture through the eyes of the judgment of the church. Some of them acted as if the Protestant

Reformation never happened or redefined it as an unimportant blip of history. Anglo-catholics continued to uphold the Thirty-Nine Articles as authoritative, but they reinterpreted them to fit their high church perspective.[19] Those who see themselves as "high church" are especially wedded to the doctrine of "Apostolic Succession." For them, Apostolic Succession is more than the "succession of teaching" that evangelicals believe; it is the continuous succession of a line of bishops that is traceable all the way back to the original apostles. They also subscribe to the doctrine of "baptismal regeneration" — the idea that everyone is automatically born again when they are baptized, whether or not grace is sought for or, in faith, received. The Tractarian fathers were not at first ritualists, but before long Medieval Catholic elements in worship and ceremony found their way back into the church. This included calling the communion table an "altar," and such practices as wearing Eucharistic vestments, making the sign of the cross at the absolution and final blessing, mixing water with wine in the chalice, and reverencing the altar (bowing) on entering or leaving the sanctuary. After 1976, as a result of the practice of ordaining women and the revision of the Prayer Book in 1979, different Anglo-catholics pulled out of the Episcopal Church to start their own breakaway churches and denominations.

RATIONALISTS trace their identity back to the 18th century Enlightenment and to the idea that human reasoning can explain everything, including matters of faith. From this came the critical study of Scripture ("Biblical Criticism") whose original purpose was to understand what the authors of Scripture were saying to the particular audiences for which they wrote. In 1889 a collection of essays was published by a group of Oxford Anglican scholars under the title *Lux mundi*.[20] This book sought to relate faith to "modern intellectual and moral problems," but its impact was to open the Anglican door to the new critical view of Holy Scripture.

Their original goal is commendable because all serious students want to find the original intent of the biblical authors. But inordinate confidence in human reasoning leads to a diminished view of divine mystery and away from the idea of revealed truth. And this can lead to the kind of cynical skepticism that casts doubt on the trustworthiness of the Bible to convey an accurate and historical picture of Jesus Christ. The more extreme rationalists consider the miracles in the Bible as no more believable than fairytales for not standing the test of reason — after all, walking on water or healing a blind man clearly breaks the laws of physical science! The Bible was seen less and less as "divine revelation" with Jesus Christ as its uniting thread,[21] and increasingly it was considered as just a collection of books without any real connection to one another.

Rationalism gradually influenced some key evangelicals and this gave birth to the "Broad Church" movement in the later half of the 19th century. Broad churchmanship tends to interpret Christianity in the light of unrestrained confidence in social progress and a "sunnier picture of human nature."[22] The extremely high anthropology of the movement tends to diminish and reinterpret the cross, making it an example of sacrificial love rather than an atoning sacrifice. Modern-day rationalists (i.e., liberals, revisionists, or progressives) have dominated the teaching in most Episcopal seminaries and the leadership in the national church for some decades. Their willingness to sometimes abandon the plain teaching of Holy Scripture in the name of "dynamic orthodoxy" or "progressivism" threatens the foundations of what Episcopalians have always believed. It has even led some to abandon the basic tenets of the creed. Liberalism, once a moniker for open-mindedness and the charitable consideration of other beliefs, has become a party label for a dogmatic and often-intolerant worldview governed by cultural trends and "what feels good."

In recent times, evangelicals and Anglo-catholics have joined efforts, for the sake of traditional Christianity, to combat liberalism's stronghold on the church. Someone said that "Feuding brothers stop feuding when a maniac invades their house."[23] The common enemy is not human reason, but the kind of "rationalism" that makes little or no room for divine revelation (i.e., the Bible) — the kind that says, "We've grown beyond the Bible's usefulness."[24]

Such neat and tidy categories (as evangelical, high church, and rationalist) are helpful to a point, but they beg the question of where to fit charismatics, social activists, the guy in the plaid sports coat who purports to subscribe to the best in each of the parties, and lots of other Episcopalian concerns. Nevertheless, they generally describe the main parties of theological reflection that make up the Episcopal Church.

DISCUSSION QUESTIONS

1. What makes Episcopalians "Anglican" and connects them to the Church of England?

2. Discuss the strengths and weaknesses of rational, evangelical, and high church parties.

3. Would Episcopalians say that "bishops" are:
    a. Absolutely necessary for church order.
    b. Not necessary, but helpful for church order.
    c. Not important at all.
    d. Look nice in church pictures (after all, what's circumstance without pomp?). (See: "The Examination" p. 517, "Ministry of Bishops" p. 855, Article "D" p. 878)

4. What is the "popular" impression of the Episcopal Church in the media and culture? How do these impressions line up with Anglican history?

5. Which of the "theological movements" do you most identify with and why?

Chapter 3

Believe it or not . . .

I eavesdropped on a conversation once in which a very nice lady said, "I love the Episcopal Church because you can believe anything and still be an Episcopalian!" Was she right? Does the Episcopal Church stand for anything? Or nothing? Episcopalians do put a premium on freedom — the freedom to use our minds, wrestle with the issues, and come to a *personal* faith. In fact, if you are looking for a church that will spoon-feed you their doctrine or tell you how to think, the Episcopal Church is not for you. This doesn't mean, however, that we stand for nothing. The church that stands for nothing will fall for anything! Within the "roominess" of the Episcopal Church is a rich heritage that defines the perimeters of Episcopal beliefs.

First and foremost, the Episcopal Church believes the Bible and believes in the Bible. We are the product of the 16th century English Reformation whose primary purpose was to return the church to the Bible as our highest authority. But this doesn't mean that we are fundamentalists. Fundamentalists invented the terms "infallibility" and "inerrancy" to convey their commitment to the inspired authorship of the Bible, but in the process they sometimes overlooked its human aspects. Theological liberals, at the other extreme, tend to emphasize the human authorship while neglecting its divine origin and inspiration. They tend to discount the miracles and any connection there is between the sixty-six books of the Bible based on the single authorship of the Holy Spirit. Episcopalians have historically maintained a balance between these two views. We believe that real human beings wrote the Bible with evidence of their humanity found throughout. We also believe that God inspired them and blessed them in their writing to accurately communicate God's Word. This honoring of dual authorship (God and man) is what distinguishes Episcopalians from many other denominations. What an incredible miracle it is, for example, that John's personality and his *fisherman's understanding* of the Greek language is found in the book of Revelation, and yet we still believe that God stands behind this book as its author and inspiration. It would have been a lesser miracle (and, no doubt, better grammar!) had God bypassed John's humanity to physically take his hand and make him write every letter.

In the Episcopal Church the Bible is always and everywhere upheld as the primary authority for determining theology and morals. "The primacy of Scripture means that Scripture is the norm of faith and the norm by which other norms (creeds, tradition, confessions of faith) are judged."[25] Prayer Book revisions, for example, are allowed so long as "there be not any thing in it contrary to the Word of God" (Prayer Book, p. 10). We believe that God "caused" the Holy Scriptures to be written for our learning (see Collect Proper 28, p. 236). Every person ordained in this church declares in writing their allegiance to the Bible "to be the Word of God, and to contain all things necessary to salvation" (p. 526). In the Catechism, we learn why the Scriptures are called the Word of God: "because God inspired their human authors and because God still speaks to us through the Bible" (p. 853). Furthermore, the Prayer Book's standard for "truth" is: "that which accords with the Scriptures" (p. 853). The Episcopal Church is also known as a "creedal church" insomuch as the creeds (Apostles and Nicene) "may be proved by most certain warrants of Holy Scripture" (Article VIII, p. 869). And lastly, a huge portion of the Episcopal Prayer Book liturgy is taken from the Bible, much of the time word-for-word.

Some in the Episcopal Church are fond of talking about three sources of authority — Scripture, reason and tradition — as a "three-legged stool." The idea is that each leg is equally important and each is a necessary counter-balance for the other two. This tidy division of authority is valuable in one respect: it shows that Episcopalians highly value reason and tradition. But, in fact, the idea of three equally weighted sources of authority is a modern invention that distorts what Episcopalians have always believed. Richard Hooker (1545-1600), our most noted theologian and called "the inventor of Anglicanism,"[26] never used the analogy of a stool as some falsely claim. And he didn't speak of three equally weighted sources of authority. He did write about three woven cords (Scripture, reason, and tradition), but he consistently spoke of the primacy of Holy Scripture.[27] An analogy better fitting our Anglican heritage is recommended by Nashota House Seminary Dean, Robert Munday: three ascending levels of a tower. He says, "Scripture is the foundation. Tradition rests on Scripture and is built upon it but cannot go where there is no foundation. Reason rests on Scripture and tradition and builds upon it but, again, cannot go where there is no supporting foundation."[28] The Bible is for Episcopalians today what it has always been: our primary source of authority. And reason and tradition (and experience) are given to help us understand and apply God's Word to our lives.

It has also been said that Episcopalians "believe what we pray" (*Lex orandi,* lex credendi — the law of praying is the law of belief). The idea is that the core of our beliefs is to be found embedded in our prayers. But this is a recent idea that "has nothing to do with anything distinctly Anglican."[29] In fact, we have always believed that prayers should reflect the truth of God's Word and not the other way around. Permission is given, for example, for periodically revising the Prayer Book, but with the proviso that the core doctrine (i.e., "essence of the faith") remains the same (p. 10).

It is commonly said that the Episcopal Church is *not* a "confessional church." This means that, unlike Lutherans who have the Augsburg Confession and Presbyterians who have the Westminster Confession, we do not have a single defining statement of belief. But this doesn't tell the whole story. Even though we are not "confessional" in quite the same way, we do have the "Articles of Religion" (sometimes called "The Thirty-Nine Articles", pp. 867-876). These were written at the same time as the other great confessions with the same purpose in mind. The 1571 (and final) version of the Articles succinctly stated their purpose: "For the avoiding of diversities of opinions and for the establishing of Consent touching true religion."[30] It is clear that the original intent of the Articles was to establish the limits of Anglican comprehensiveness at a time when Protestant extremists ("Anabaptists") and the Church of Rome were competing for a place in the English church. The Articles have enjoyed widespread and consistent support as our key doctrinal statement.[31] At the General Convention of 1801 the fledgling American Episcopal Church adopted the Articles as its theological standard.

Another historical document that helps define what Episcopalians believe is the Chicago-Lambeth Quadrilateral of 1888 (p. 877). Starting in 1867 and roughly every ten years since then, Anglican bishops from all over the world have gathered at the invitation of the Archbishop of Canterbury to talk about the common concerns of the Communion (called Lambeth Conferences). The 1888 Lambeth Conference revised four Articles first agreed to by the House of Bishops of the Episcopal Church (Chicago 1886). Both houses of General Convention (the House of Bishops and the House of Deputies) approved the current language in 1895. These four affirmations are pillars of Anglicanism for discussions about reuniting the Christian Church. Holy Scripture is the ultimate standard of faith, the two creeds are sufficient statements of Christian Faith, the two great sacraments are Baptism and Holy Communion, and bishops have a historic place in the Christian Church.

A plaque in my office has this saying: ***In essentials - unity; in non-essentials - liberty; and in all things - charity***. This is Episcopalianism! It's a room big enough for lots of dialogue and different ideas, but its parameters are defined by certain essentials (i.e., biblical truth as it is summarized in the creeds, the Prayer Book, and "Articles of Religion"). The preface of the Prayer Book makes the important distinction between "doctrine" and "discipline" (pp. 9-11). Discipline includes those matters that can and should change from time to time to make the church relevant to modern language and culture. This includes the words of our worship and prayers, and the moral and theological matters that the Bible doesn't address. Doctrine, on the other hand, is the "substance of the faith" that is true today as it has always been (Jude 3 "the faith once and for all delivered"). Doctrine includes the moral teaching on the many issues where the Bible is abundantly clear. Doctrine doesn't change over time because it is the core biblical teaching that is always true, always relevant, and always contemporary — "the grass withers, the flower fades; but the word of our God will stand forever" (Isa. 40:8).

The nice lady I overheard was wrong. The most dangerous threat today to Episcopal identity is the church's infatuation with "tolerance."[32] It sometimes seems more important to be polite than truthful, to celebrate our differences than to assert that we know something with confidence. Diversity, once only a description of the colorful variety that makes up our Church, has seemingly become the objective of our faith. A bishop I once heard said that it is better to be loving than correct. This must be true, as far as it goes. But the best is to be loving **and correct**. In fact, something cannot be really "loving" unless it is based in "truth" ("Love rejoices in the truth" 1 Cor. 13:6). To pursue unity at the expense of the truth does not lead to unity in the church, but unity of the church to the world.[33] Jesus said that the **Truth** will make us free (John 8:32), not some hollow senti-mentalism that embraces every teaching that comes down the road. Hope for the Episcopal Church lies in the possibility of a humble awakening to our history that is founded on the enduring truth of God's Word.

DISCUSSION QUESTIONS:

1. Look up the cited Prayer Book references in this chapter and discuss how the Prayer Book addresses the question of "authority" in determining matters of theology and ethics.

2. What distinguishes Episcopalians from other denominations in our respective views of the Bible?

3. Read: 2 Timothy 3:16,17; 2 Peter 1:20,21; John 3:34, 6:63; Joshua 1:8; Psalm 1; Psalm 119:105 and discuss what the Bible claims of itself.

4. A favorite Bible story often cited for teaching unlimited tolerance is John 8:1-11. Was Jesus loving at the expense of truth?

5. What's the difference between "doctrine" and "discipline" (see Preface to the Prayer Book, p. 9-11). The Preface was first published in the 1789 Prayer Book and has been in every Episcopal revision since then.

6. Review each of the four Articles of the 1888 Lambeth Quadrilateral (p. 877), making reference where helpful to the teachings of the "Outline of the Faith" (pp. 845-62).

Chapter 4

What's so good about this news?

S o, WHAT do Episcopalians believe? That's a big question that would include how we view God, our relationship with creation, and how we conduct our lives. There's obviously not enough space here to begin to address these things, but we can identify the heart of the matter. We call it "the Gospel" or Good News. And the heart of the gospel is not what some will think. It's not primarily the life of Christ or his teaching or his exhortations for Christians to get along with one another. The heart of the Christian message is **the cross**.[34]

The Apostle Paul said, "May I never boast of anything except the cross of our Lord Jesus Christ" (Gal 6:14). This is the thread, the master theme, which unites the whole Bible. The Old Testament foretells and the New Testament explained that Jesus "truly suffered, was crucified, dead, and buried, to reconcile his Father to us . . ." (Article II, p. 868).[35] On a human level the cross is gruesome and bloody. But the Bible tells us that it is absolutely central to God's plan for salvation.

Jesus died on the cross to save us. But saved from what? And how did he do it? There are many ways to explain the Gospel, but any attempt that doesn't include at least something about these four elements will be incomplete: God, human nature, Jesus Christ, and our response.

GOD

Lots of things can be said about God, but these two things are essential: he is holy and he is loving. "Note then the kindness and severity of God . . ." (Rom. 11:22).

God is holy. He is not "like us, only better." He is absolutely morally pure and free from sin and imperfection. God existed before time was invented and his kingdom will have no end. His word is so powerful that by just speaking he brought everything into being from nothing. He never changes in His almighty power, wisdom, and justice that utterly surpasses our ability to comprehend. By his nature he detests sin and everything that is a contradiction to his holiness. And since he is holy, God has made holiness the condition required for salvation. The Bible tells us that God is angry (wrathful) at sinful, self-centered humanity who set themselves against his plans and purposes. His is a holy anger, not a flying-off-the-handle kind. His anger is only appeased by righteousness: people and all of creation restored to a right relationship with God.

God is love. He acts lovingly, but it's more than that. So thoroughly is this his nature that the Bible says that Jesus *is* love (1 John 4:16). And the best news of all is that his love is personal. The creator of all that exists knows the number of hairs on your head, and every sparrow that falls. He calls each of us by name! Even though we do not deserve it, he loves us. Even when we're at our worst, he never stops. No one, no matter how badly they've managed their lives, is beyond the reach of his love and forgiveness. The word for this highest of all loves is "grace." The Bible tells us that God is like the father of a completely rude and disrespectful son (Luke 15). The son demanded his inheritance and then wasted it all on wild living. The father had every right to be furious, but the day he saw his son walking down the road toward home, he forgot to be angry because of his joy over his son's return. God's love is his dominant attribute and the reason why he sent his only Son.[36] God is always ready to welcome us home, to forgive our sins and extend to us the gift of a personal relationship. To know God's love is to enter into that special place of eternal security found only in the arms of our Heavenly Father.

HUMAN NATURE

"Magnificence" and the "misery" are the two things that we must know about the human condition. We are made in God's image *and* we are miserable sinners.

According to the Bible, humans are the pinnacle of creation, created in God's own image to share his glory (Gen. 1:27). Someone once calculated that the chemicals in a human body are worth just a few dollars. Yet the Bible teaches that this arrangement of chemicals has immeasurable value to God. Unique in all of creation, humans are created to live in friendship with God. At the very least this means that we are more than flesh and bones; we have a living soul and God's life is breathed into us. Adam and Eve, the first humans, are pictured as strolling in the garden and chatting with God as friends. To be created in his image means that we have the God-given capacity (but not the guarantee) to relate to God as children to a father. Our highest purpose on earth is to enjoy this relationship.

But just as the Bible teaches that we are created in God's image, it also teaches that the creation was quickly followed by the entry of evil into human hearts (Gen. 3). When Adam and Eve disobeyed God (i.e., "the Fall"), evil effects came to all creation. Because of our connection to our most distant disobedient relatives, we are selfish, prideful, and resistant to anyone telling us what to do – including God. Our sinful bent is called "original sin." The popular view that we are just a little dirty in need of a little cleaning up is not the biblical view. St. Paul put is this way, "All have sinned and fall short of the glory of God," and "There is no one who is righteous, not even one" (Rom. 3:9, 23). In another place he writes, "You were dead in your trespasses and sins . . ." (Eph. 2:1). Even though we have the capacity to be friends with God (i.e., created in his image), we are by nature heading in another direction because of our thoroughly sinful orientation. In even our best human efforts, because we are sinners, we are unable to reach up to God and meet the requirement for righteousness. Something drastic, something earthshaking, had to happen from outside of us in order for us to have hope to heal our relationship with God.[37]

JESUS CHRIST

The central theme of the Bible is the coming of Jesus to save men and women from sin. Only someone who is fully God and fully man could do this. These are the two most important things to know about Jesus.

The baby born in Bethlehem's barn 2,000 years ago was a real human being. It's mind-boggling to think that Jesus dirtied his diapers and wailed when he was hungry like every baby. He had human emotions — love, sorrow, anger, and compassion. The Bible tells us that he experienced hunger, thirst, and sometimes sheer exhaustion. Although throughout his ministry he experienced prophetic insights and supernatural knowledge not experienced by everyone, he also showed his full humanity by asking real questions, felt a need to pray regularly, and was tempted in every way that we are. It was real blood that came from his pain-racked body on the cross. Yet, in the fullness of his humanity, the Scriptures tell us (amazingly!) that he never sinned.

It's incredible to think that the baby that needed the touch and comfort of his mother was his mother's Maker and Savior! Jesus was flesh-and-bones man, but also God. "Immanuel" means "God with us." He existed before he took on human form from the beginning, before there was time or creation. One day, in the course of human history, he stepped out of his home in heaven to become one of us. "The Word became flesh and lived among us" (John 1:14). He did this to show that he would do anything and everything to reach us and save us. He temporarily and voluntarily "emptied Himself" of divine prerogatives to become a full human being (Phil. 2). But he never gave up being God even for a minute.

How then could the holy love of God come to terms with the unholy sinfulness of men and women? The answer — in fact the only answer — is the cross. The only way God could simultaneously express his holiness and love was by providing a substitute. And the only possible substitute was the One who is both God and man. Jesus was born to die. That's why almost half of each of the gospels is devoted to the last few days of his life and the crucifixion. Instead of imposing on us the punishment we deserved, God in Christ endured it for us. Jesus took on himself the full weight of God's holy wrath so that we could be restored to a right relation-ship with God. He bridged the gap caused by our sin. So completely was he our substitute on the cross, according to the Bible he actually "became sin" (literally "became the sin-bearer") so that "in him we might become the righteousness of God" (2 Cor. 5:21). Paul put it this way, "Christ redeemed us from the curse of the law by becoming a curse for us" (Gal. 3:13). In Peter's first letter he wrote: "He himself bore our sins in his body on the cross . . ." (2:24). And the writer of Hebrews said Christ was "offered once to bear the sins of many" (9:28).

The Bible teaches that Jesus' death and resurrection had cosmic dimensions. Not only did he pay the full price for our salvation, but he once and for all won victory over evil and the powers of the devil. "The Son of God was revealed for this purpose, to destroy the works of the devil" (1 John 3:8). In another place John wrote that the ruler of this world has been condemned" (John 16:11). And the writer of Hebrews added, "that through [Christ's] death he might destroy the one who has the power of death, that is, the devil" (2:14).

This is how much God loves us! Such is his grace! We can be forgiven of our sins because Jesus died for us. We can leave our self-centeredness and begin a new life with God because, through his death and resurrec-tion, he has opened the way.

SO WHAT?

To know this gospel intellectually is one thing; to believe it in our minds and hearts will save us. You must accept God's free gift of salvation and agree to follow him as Lord in order to be saved and have eternal life.

Religion never saved anyone. Christianity, at its heart, is not a religion but a relationship. Some people call themselves "Christians," and may even look like Christians on the outside, but they don't have a personal relationship with God. Their spirits are not alive to God by action of the Holy Spirit. It requires a decision on our part, an act of the will, to live into our inheritance. We could be the beneficiaries of a million dollars and still live in poverty because we have not cashed the check. Paul in

Romans writes, "If you confess with your lips that Jesus is Lord and believe in your heart that God raised him from the dead, you will be saved" (10:9). Then he went on to make what was simple even simpler: "Everyone who calls on the name of the Lord shall be saved" (v. 13). John says it this way: "To all who receive him, who believe in his name, he gave the power to become children of God" (John 1:12).

If you are a new inquirer to the Episcopal Church or even an old-time member, please be absolutely clear that God's gift of salvation is different from being a good person, or the same thing as being baptized or becoming a member of a church. It's possible to be humanitarian-of-the-year, for Billy Graham himself to have baptized you, and to be a leader in your church and still be spiritually dead. Nicodemus (John 3) was an outstanding example of a really good and religious person. In fact, we would be hard-pressed to come up with a better example of a truly good human being. But to such a man Jesus said, "You must be born again!" If Nicodemus needed that experience, how much more do we! It's not what we do for God that counts for salvation, but what he has done for us. Have you confessed your need? Asked him to forgive your sins? To fill your life with his holy and life-giving Spirit? Have you committed yourself to follow him as your Lord? If you haven't and would like to — if you feel that God has brought you to this critical point in your life and that the spiritual hunger you are feeling is God urging you to accept him — you can do it right now. In your heart of hearts you can pray a prayer like this:

Lord Jesus Christ,
I admit that I have sinned and gone my own way.
Please forgive me, not because I deserve to be forgiven,
but because you died on the cross to take away my sins.
I am willing for you to lead and direct my life from now on.
I open my heart to receive you.
Fill me with your holy and life-giving Spirit.
I receive you as my Savior and Friend and Lord forever.
AMEN.[38]

Like some of you, I grew up in the Episcopal Church and I have lots of good memories. But I don't remember a time as a child or as a young person hearing the gospel explained. And I can't remember a time in Sunday school or in a church service when I was invited to accept God's free gift of salvation. It was only later that I accepted Jesus as my Lord and Savior and began a heart-felt relationship with him. And it was much later that I realized, *to my utter surprise*, that this gospel message is something so deeply "Episcopalian" that we hear it every single Sunday in our worship service. See if you can identify the elements (p. 362)?

<u>God</u>	holy and loving
<u>Human Nature</u>	God's image and sinners
<u>Jesus Christ</u>	God and man (our substitute)
<u>So What?</u>	receive and follow as Lord

Holy and *gracious* Father: In your infinite love *you made us for yourself*; and, when *we had fallen* into sin and become subject to evil and death, you, in your mercy, sent Jesus Christ, your only and *eternal Son*, to share our *human nature*, to live and die as one of us, *to reconcile us to you, the God and Father of all.*

DISCUSSION QUESTIONS

1. Read the Bible passages cited for the four parts of the gospel message
    and discuss their meaning:
    God
    Holy - Isaiah 6:3; Nahum 1:2-8; Romans 1:18, 5:9
    Love - I John 4:16; Romans 8:38-39; John 3:16

    Human Nature
    In His Image - Genesis 1:26; Psalm 8:5-6;
    Sinful - Genesis 3:7; Romans 3:10, 3:23, 8:22; Ephesians 2:1

    Jesus Christ
    God - John 1:1, 14:9; Matthew 27:54
    Man - Philippians 2:6-11; Isaiah 53:5; Romans 5:8, Mark 10:45

    Our Response (So What?)
    Receive - Ephesians 2:8; Acts 16:31
    Follow as Lord - Ephesians 1:22; Philippians 2:10,11; John 15:10

2. How are the theological terms found in this chapter defined: gospel,
    holiness, sin, the Fall, original sin, redemption, righteousness,
    and grace?

3. How did you come into a living relationship with Jesus Christ?
    If you have not yet made a decision for Christ, what keeps you
    from doing so?

Chapter 5
Messiah of the month club

The setting was a college campus and the speaker was fiery and adamant. "Who would be so ignorant as to believe that Jesus is the *only* way to God?" The Episcopal bishop went on to say, "Such a judgment would obviously exclude millions of respectable and moral Jews, Hindus, and Muslims — the majority of the human race! This exclusivity would be totally out of character with a loving God." Then he drove the point home with the ever-popular: "All roads lead to God and we must respect one another."[39] As you might imagine, the college audience indicated their approval with enthusiastic applause.

The idea that all religions more or less say the same thing or represent different paths to the same God is generally accepted today. "Pluralism," as it's called, says that it doesn't matter *what* you believe as long as you are sincere. This appeals to our Episcopalian sensitivities that value politeness very highly. And the reluctance to say that we know anything with certainty, what one theologian calls "a fashionable preference for doubt,"[40] excuses us from responsibility to objective truth and leaves us with only the subjective kind that says, 'Christianity is true *for me*.'

Is the bishop right? Is Jesus one of many ways? Or did God reveal himself fully and decisively in Jesus Christ alone? What *do* Episcopalians believe?

To begin with, everyone should know that tolerance as a virtue has obvious limits. No one would tolerate a dog that bites everyone it meets, and an abused wife who tolerates her husband's beatings is to be pitied, not commended. And it's also obvious that different religions are really

31

different. Who would argue that Christianity and animism and Satanism are equally valid responses to God? Christianity and Islam, two of the world's great religions, are also clearly different. To take just one example: the New Testament is emphatic that Jesus died on the cross, and the Qur'an, the Muslim bible, is equally emphatic that he did not. These are foundational teachings of both faiths and both can't be true. Furthermore, how are all religions basically the same if their goals are patently different? Christians hope for resurrection to everlasting life; Hindus envision reincarnation; and Rastafarians look forward to paradise where blacks are served by menial whites. To ignore the glaring differences might seem broad-minded, but in fact it is the worst kind of narrow-mindedness. To assert that all religions are essentially the same is a slap in the face to millions of people around the world who see the distinctives of their religion as critical. Christians should humbly and lovingly respect people of all faiths and work with them where we can for the goals that we share. But there's a big difference between respecting other religions and regarding all of them as equally valid roads leading to a common salvation.

God is not squeamish about distinctions even if we are. Scripture teaches unequivocally that followers of other religions are being led by deceptive spirits who oppose the God who created them and loves them.[41] For example, the first two of the Ten Commandments — have no other gods, make no idols — show that God regards it a serious offense to become involved in other religions. "I will bring judgment on all the gods of Egypt," he said, and "Do not go after other gods" (Exod.12:12; Jer. 35:15). In addition, the Bible is unembarrassed to make extraordinary claims about the uniqueness of Jesus and to assert his superiority over other gods. This is what those who met him said about him: "Never has anyone spoken like this!" (John 7:46), "Lord, to whom shall we go? You have the words of eternal life" (John 6:68), "Go away from me, Lord, for I am a sinful man!" (Luke 5:8), "Who then is this, that even the wind and sea obey him?" (Mark 4:41), "You are the Messiah, the Son of the living God" (Matt.16:16), and "My Lord and my God!" (John 20:28).[42]

Not only does the Bible teach that Jesus is "the only begotten Son of God" (words of the Nicene Creed), it also teaches that he is the only way to salvation. On the day of Pentecost Peter preached that "there is salvation in no one else, for there is no other name under heaven given among mortals by which we must be saved" (Acts 4:12). Jesus himself said, "I am the way, and the truth, and the life. No one comes to the Father except through me" (John 14:6). And Paul said, "there is one God; there is also one mediator between God and humankind, Christ Jesus . . . who gave himself as ransom for all" (1 Tim. 2:5). Anglican theologian Michael Green wrote, "Our forefathers in the faith died for their witness to the uniqueness and supremacy of Jesus as Lord and Savior. It is not for us to betray them and him in our generation."[43]

"Grace" is the unmerited and undeserved love of God for sinners, and it's what sets Christianity apart from all other faiths. Christians have a Savior and a salvation unlike all others. Are there other saviors who love humans with perfect constancy even when they're behaving badly? Is there another god who invested himself so fully in humankind that he became one of us to rescue us? Is there another savior who washed his disciples' feet or willingly submitted to death on a cross? Is there another salvation that is based on the certainty of God's goodness rather than ours? Only Christianity teaches that God in Christ saved the world for those who haven't earned it, can't do enough to earn it, and would never have a hope for salvation if God hadn't stepped in to remedy the situation. "See what love the father has given us that we should be called the children of God!"(1 John 3:15). No other religion teaches that we are saved because God loves us beyond our wildest imaginations.

But some take the idea of "grace" and stretch it to say that everyone will be saved and go to heaven. They can't bring themselves to believe that God's love would ever exclude anyone. This is called "universalism." The Bible does teach that Jesus died for everyone and that his love is universal (John 3:16; 1 Tim. 2:4). But it also teaches that entrance into his kingdom requires an act of faith — personally accepting God's gift. As Oxford theologian Alister McGrath said, "it is a small step from the optimistic affirmation that 'all will be saved' to the authoritarian pronouncement that 'all must be saved' — whether they like it or not."[44] He went on to say that salvation is meaningful only because we have the right (free will) to refuse it, and universalism denies people the right to say "no" to God. The same Bible that teaches us about heaven also teaches that God will send to hell those who decide to go there, those who refuse his free gift of salvation. C. S. Lewis said that "there are only two kinds of people in the end: those who say to God, 'Thy will be done," and those to whom God says, in the end, 'Thy will be done.' All that are in Hell, choose it."[45] Universalism is an understanding based on wishful thinking, not on the Word of God.

The Bible's exclusive claim that God has revealed himself fully and decisively in Jesus Christ causes heartburn in some circles. But there are only a few options for Christians: we can dismiss the Bible entirely as a dusty old book without relevance for today; or we can selectively apply its meaning to say that it is simply mistaken and culturally bound on this subject; or we can accept it as God's true plan and purpose that should shape what we believe. If we take the Bible seriously, there's no getting around what it says about Jesus.

Episcopalians, then, are both inclusive and exclusive. We believe that Jesus died for everyone's sins, not just for Christians, and he desires everyone to be saved (1 Timothy 2:4), not wanting any to perish (2 Peter 3:9), so that he may be merciful to all (Romans 11:32). But we also believe that there is only one way to salvation: "For Scripture doth set out unto us only the Name of Jesus Christ, whereby men must be saved" (Article XVIII, p. 871). Even though we believe that Jesus is the only way to God, this doesn't mean that we are ready to condemn to hell those who have not heard the gospel. Only God will finally determine who's in and who's out. Only God is judge, and I'm sure that there will be surprises when we get to heaven. Once when Jesus was asked if many would be saved, he basically said, "That's up to me; just make sure you are in!" (my loose interpretation of Luke 13:23).

What then are we to think about our family members and friends who don't personally know Jesus Christ as their Lord? What if your brother follows another religion or your boss is an atheist? Understandably, the last thing we want is to be judgmental or condemning. Christian claims about the exclusive nature of salvation are hard for many people, especially in our western culture where there are few values more important than tolerance and diversity. But if it's true that God has provided the way to be reconciled with our Creator, and true that on this matter very literally hinges the question of where someone will spend eternity, we would be the most selfish people in the world to not share the life-changing message of Jesus Christ. It's not a superior attitude, but a loving and longing heart that drives Christian evangelism. It's not that Christians are better than anyone else, but we serve the world as one beggar telling other beggars where we found bread.[46]

Are all religions one? No, clearly not! The fiery Episcopal bishop was mistaken about one of the central teachings of Christianity. The uniqueness of Jesus Christ, called the "scandal of particularity,"[47] is anything but scandalous to those who are spiritually hungry, who are looking for God's remedy for the hunger they feel.

DISCUSSION QUESTIONS

1. What makes Christianity unique among the world's religions?

2. What response can you think of for the next time someone tells you that all religions worship the same God, or all roads lead to the same salvation?

3. Read and discuss the "context" (or setting) for these verses: Acts 4:12; John 14:6; and 1 Timothy 2:5.

4. Read and discuss the meaning of Article XVIII, p. 871.

5. What's the difference between evangelism and imposing your views on people?

6. Do you know someone who is spiritually lost? What can you do to help them to God?

Chapter 6

Sin, not promiscuous genes

Several years ago a bishop in Scotland announced that some people have a "gene" that predisposes them to commit adultery — a promiscuous gene. When the word hit the press Alleluias could be heard around the world! This revelation of the Primate [i.e., the head bishop] of the Episcopal Church in Scotland, Richard Holloway, was welcome news for everyone looking for a way to explain the lipstick stains on their shirt collars! Is he right? Can we not help ourselves? There is certainly something that predisposes us to have multiple sex partners, but what is it? What Bishop Holloway blames on biology is really caused by sin.

Even if genes have something to do with our moral makeup (a proposition still being studied), this doesn't mean that we are helpless victims. There is a higher authority than, "I felt the urge!" Urges, impulses, and giddy feelings are notoriously unreliable sources for determining God's will. Just because a person feels the urge to steal, get drunk, or slap their spouse around doesn't make it right any more than the urge to commit adultery makes that right. The temptations may be strong, even very strong, but we always have a choice to live for the promises we made in our wedding vows. What differentiates animals from human beings, after all, is that animals (and apparently a few priests and bishops!)[48] are ruled by their appetites and do not yield to a higher standard. The Apostle Paul assures us that "God is faithful, and he will not let you be tested beyond your strength, but with the testing he will also provide the way out so that you may be able to endure it" (1 Cor. 10:13).

Should we revise our ethics to accommodate the victims of promiscuous genes? Is there an "Episcopalian" way of addressing ethical questions? What standard do we use to determine right from wrong?

First, if you want a list of acceptable and unacceptable behaviors you will be disappointed in the Episcopal Church. Occasionally dioceses and General Conventions will make (unbinding and sometimes bizarre) moral pronouncements,[49] but, other than the Bible, we don't have an official code for moral conduct. Our goal is less to tell Episcopalians how to act, than to encourage them to have Christian (i.e., biblical) minds and world-views, and to act accordingly. Unlike some other denominations, we give strong deference to an individuals' ability to make personal moral choices based on the sources of authority available to them. This means that Episcopalians sometimes differ among themselves about certain issues. What is constant, however, is the methodology that guides our considera-tions. The same Anglican/Episcopalian methodology that guides the study of theology also guides moral theology. Namely, the Bible is the primary authority, and reason and tradition are helpful in understanding and applying God's Word to our lives. For someone to reach a determination about the morality of war or abortion or premarital sex, to be "Episcopalian," it will have the support of Scripture, reason, and tradition.

Using "adultery" as an example, is there a consistent and clear teach-ing about this in the Bible? Yes, the Bible plainly says that marriage is a life-long monogamous union of a man and woman (Gen. 2:24; Matt. 19:4-6). Even though early civilizations, including the Israelites, practiced polygamy, the Bible consistently moves toward one-man-one-woman rela-tionships as God's highest plan. It prohibits all sexual relations outside of marriage (e.g., Exod. 20:14, Matt. 5:27-28), and it uniformly calls adulter-ous relationships "sinful" (e.g., John 8:3). There is no wavering in the bibli-cal teaching about this. Nowhere is adultery shown in a positive light, and everywhere it is condemned as wrong. The church throughout history has upheld this interpretation (tradition), and the social sciences confirm that adultery is destructive to families and other social institutions (reason).

Can a bishop then, even the Primate of the Episcopal Church in Scotland, approve of such a practice? Not unless he is willing to leave the parameters of what the Episcopal Church teaches. And any bishop who finds himself or herself outside the teaching of the church should resign or be booted out by their fellow bishops.

The same methodology of considering the Bible, reason, and tradition can be used to evaluate every moral issue. But what about the Bible? Who hasn't heard, "the Bible doesn't condemn homosexuality (or any other controversial issue), it's just how you interpret it." This suggests that the Bible can be used to support just about any point of view — *so why bother?* If the Bible is the primary authority for Episcopalians, how can someone read and interpret it with confidence for discerning God's will? Over Christian history a consensus of helpful principles has emerged.

The first is **the principle of inspiration**. Episcopalians affirm the Bible as God's inspired Word — he "caused the Holy Scriptures to be written for our learning" (p. 236). And the best interpreter of any book is its author. When we read the Bible we consider that it's "from God" and we seek to live in line with its teaching. We ask the Holy Spirit's help so that we can understand it. The Holy Spirit enlightens those who are spiritually alive: "Those who are unspiritual do not receive the gifts of God's Spirit, for they are foolishness to them, and they are unable to understand them because they are spiritually discerned" (1 Cor. 2:14). He enlightens the humble: ". . . You have hidden these from the wise and intelligent and have revealed them to infants" (Matt. 11:25). And lastly, the Holy Spirit enlightens those who are willing to obey: "Anyone who resolves to do the will of God will know whether the teaching is from God or whether I am speaking on my own" (John 7:17). As we approach the Bible we want to have the same attitude as the Psalmist: "Open my eyes so that I can see what you show me of your miracle-wonders. I'm a stranger to these parts; give me your clear directions" (Ps. 119:18 *The Message*, Eugene Peterson).

The second principle is **the principle of simplicity**. This is the practice of looking for the natural or plain meaning of the text. The Bible is a revelation not an obscuration, and God's purpose is to lead us to truth not boggle our minds. Therefore, we will interpret a passage considering its literary type: history as history, poetry as poetry, and allegory as allegory. Lots of mistakes are made when we assume one literary type for the whole Bible (e.g., forcing a historical, scientific view on Genesis 1-11, or assuming the New Testament is poetry/myth with a few hard-to-find glimpses of the real historic Jesus thrown in). The natural meaning is not necessarily the literal meaning – Jesus is not literally sitting on God's right hand, and he is not a literal wooden door of a sheepfold. And parables are stories of common everyday scenes that are meant to tell us something about the Kingdom of God. They are meant to shake us into realizing some great truth about God, not to be dissected and significance assigned to every little detail. This is the impact they would have had for those who first heard them. The principle of simplicity requires that we interpret Scripture based on the most natural meaning of a text.

The third is **the principle of context**. As much as we can know from the surrounding verses and the overall message of a particular book, what was the author's original meaning? What did the original hearers hear and understand? Who wrote it? To whom? For what reasons? Resources, such as Bible commentaries and dictionaries can be helpful. Sometimes a passage that seems culturally bound and irrelevant is applicable today in terms of the principle behind it. For example, Paul teaches in 1 Corinthians that women are to keep their heads covered (11:5). In the first century, covering heads was a symbol of submission to authority. Even though women are obviously not expected to wear hats today, the principle related to authority still applies. Only when we have ascertained as best we can what the meaning of the passage was to the original hearers can we accurately begin to apply it to our lives today. The principle of context precludes us from imposing our modern prejudices upon the ancient text.

Another principle for Bible interpretation is **the principle of unity and harmony**. Since God stands behind the Bible as its author and inspiration we interpret it as a whole rather than as sixty-six separate books without any real connection to one another. This means first that both testaments are the Word of God and complement each other, "for both in the Old and New Testament everlasting life is offered to Mankind by Christ" (Article VII, p. 869). Additionally, it means that we will not "expound one place of Scripture, that it be repugnant to another" (Article XX, p. 871). A teaching or doctrine cannot be considered *biblical* unless it sums up and includes all that the Bible says about it. Therefore, it is unhelpful to pull out isolated verses to support our pre-formed conclusions if the verses do not account for the overall teaching. This is called "proof texting." We also believe that God progressively revealed his Word over time so that if there's tension between the older and the newer portions of Scripture, the older will give way to the newer. A good example of this is the way the Bible addresses the status of women. In older biblical cultures women were considered property and non-persons, but they were given increasing dignity and honor from ancient Israel up to the New Testament. Jesus, especially as he is seen in Luke's gospel, was the champion of "women's rights" in his day. And Paul, clearly challenging the male-dominated culture of the first century, put men and women on the same footing for salvation (e.g., Gal. 3:28). This was counter cultural and revolutionary! Many theologians feel justified in supporting women in ministry (and opposing the practice of slavery) based on the progression they see in the Bible. The principle of unity and harmony requires us to keep an eye on the overall teaching of Holy Scripture.

And the last is **the catholic principle**. An interpretation of a particular passage of Scripture can be tested for accuracy by whether or not it is supported by the theological consensus of historic Christianity. This doesn't elevate tradition to the same place as the Bible, but it looks to tradition to confirm an accurate interpretation. Vincent of Lerins, a fifth-century monk, described this as "that faith which has been believed everywhere, always, by all," and theologian Thomas Oden calls this "the ancient consensual tradition of Spirit-guided discernment of scripture."[50] The English Reformers, our Anglican forefathers, read deeply not only

41

the Bible but also the writings of the early church fathers. They believed that the same Holy Spirit who inspired the writers of Scripture protected the Word of God over time. This doesn't mean that there are no new truths to be discovered in a passage of Scripture, but it does mean that any new understandings will have to answer to the historic, consensual understanding of the passage. For example, based on the catholic principle it would be impossible to conclude that Jesus was merely a man and not the Son of God, or that the Trinity is an outdated idea, or that Mary Magdalene was Jesus' live-in girlfriend. If our study leads us to an interpretation different from the church's understanding over time, the catholic principle requires that we back up and reapproach the passage with the humility to admit that the wisdom of the ages is almost certainly better than ours.

God did not leave us in the dark about his plan for salvation, and neither does he hide his plan for how Christians are to live and conduct themselves. He gave us the Bible as our primary rule, and reason and tradition to help. The Ten Commandments and the moral teachings of Scripture are not meant to deprive us of enjoyment and fun so that we live under the heavy hand of God (Thou shall not!). Instead, they describe what our lives will look like when we are in his will. Bishop Holloway would have us believe that "because we are born this way" we are excused for our behavior. He is right in one way: we *are* born this way. But just because we are born sinners doesn't give us permission to call good what is sinful. The good news is that, in spite of our environment and genes, we can still choose to live according to God's plan.

DISCUSSION QUESTIONS

1. How do Episcopalians determine right from wrong?

2. In biblical interpretation, what is:
   a. Principle of Inspiration
   b. Principle of Simplicity
   c. Principle of Context
   d. Principle of Unity and Harmony
   e. The Catholic principle

3. How would the above principles of biblical interpretation apply to the Bible's view of homosexuality?

   Bible on human sexuality: Genesis 1:26; 2:18-24; Matthew 19:4-6

   Bible on heterosexual behavior: Song of Solomon; Proverbs 31; 1 Corinthians 7

   Bible on homosexual behavior: Genesis 19 (beginning 13:13; 18:20,21); Leviticus 18:22, 20:13; Romans 1:27-27; 1 Corinthians 6:9-10; 1 Timothy 1:9-10

Questions to help guide a discussion of the biblical issues:
A. Homosexuality is such a small issue in the Bible (about seven verses that specifically address it, and Jesus never talks about it directly), how can we claim to know God's mind in this matter?
B. How does the biblical view of marriage (God's order in creation) relate to this discussion?
C. Are there any passages that show homosexual behavior in a positive light? Is there an example of a wholesome, approved homosexual relationship?
D. Is there any wavering in the biblical witness regarding homosexual behavior?
E. Is there any evidence of a lessening in severity (progression) from Old Testament references to the New Testament?

43

Chapter 7

No "bless me" club!

Episcopalians have a unique and beautiful way of worshipping God that's based on the predictability of a Prayer Book service and the promise of meeting God in praise. Its aim is to appreciate a great God whose power and love is great enough to rescue men and women from their sins. Many find worship in the Episcopal tradition to be deeply renewing and comforting. Here are a few questions that newcomers to the Episcopal Church ask from time to time:

Why does the Episcopal Church seem so formal?

No doubt it will seem formal to some, but the goal is to be "respectful," not formal. In fact there are formal Episcopal churches (fancy vestments, organ music, etc) and informal churches (blue jeans, guitars, etc.), but the common thread is a worship tradition that is God-honoring, has encouraged the hearts of Christians for hundreds of years, and is completely biblical in its content. Worship is the experience of encountering God with an attitude of thanksgiving, and the most powerful worship happens when Christians sing and pray together in community. God lives everywhere, but he reveals his power and presence especially when Christians gather together in his name. Episcopalians are encouraged to prepare themselves to meet the Lord in worship. No one would casually and lackadaisically stroll into the office of the President of the United States; we would do so with the respect and dignity that his office commands. In the same way, Episcopalians address God not just by the first thing that comes into their heads, but with language that's noble and fitting for a King. Many kneel and pray when they first enter the church so that they can acknowledge Jesus' presence and Lordship — as you would greet the host when you first arrive at a dinner party.

Episcopal worship focuses on God, not us. We begin services with the words, "Blessed be God," not "Lord, bless me." This is notably different from the "bless me" attitude of the world and of many churches today. Some churches are designed to entertain and bless those who come — a filling station approach where the congregants go to get spiritually filled up for the week. But Episcopalians, instead, focus on God; he's the audience; he's the reason why we come to pray and sing. The Psalm invites us to "enter his presence with thanksgiving; go into his courts with praise" (Ps. 100). We come to bless God with the offering (sacrifice) of praise and thanksgiving, the giving of our lives to him. And as we do this, an amazing thing happens: we find ourselves blessed and spiritually filled for the week to come.

What is one of our greatest blessings — a Christ-centered and thoroughly biblical liturgy — can also be our greatest curse. Familiarity and repetition can breed contempt if we are not careful. Someone can say the words that for centuries have led people into the presence of God, but do it in a way that's mindless and never touches the heart. A parrot can be trained to recite the same words, but God is not impressed! There's a world of difference between a congregation that is captured by the majesty and wonder of God that's expressed so meaningfully in the Prayer Book, and one that is just going through the motions. Jesus' harshest criticism was reserved for the "religious" people of his day who, he said, "worship me with their lips, but their hearts are far from me" (Matt. 15:8). The Episcopal Church at its best has nothing to do with formalism and everything to do with the things that promote a heart-felt encounter with the living God. However mysterious and formal it may seem, all that we do in worship is meant to promote a sense of the greatness of God and the wonderful privilege of "entering his presence with thanksgiving."

Am I crazy or does Episcopal worship feel "Catholic?"

There's a historical reason for why Episcopal worship has a Catholic flavor. Like all Protestant churches, we came from the Catholic Church in the sixteenth century. The teaching of the church (i.e., tradition) had acquired a sense of being the highest authority, and the Bible was viewed as one part of tradition. This allowed the church in the Middle Ages to subscribe to some extra-biblical and even some unbiblical teachings and practices. But when the Church of England broke from Rome and redis-covered the Bible as the highest authority, we began to test the traditions of the church against the teaching of Holy Scripture. Unlike some other Protestant churches who discarded everything "Catholic" in order to start a totally new thing, we didn't throw the baby out with the bathwater. The English Settlement reflects the conscious decision to retain the Catholic practices and traditions that didn't conflict with the teaching of Holy Scripture. The result is a church that continues to have a Catholic flavor, but is thoroughly Protestant in its teaching.

Why don't you just say your prayers? Why do you read them?

Episcopalians are encouraged to pray using their own words as well as using the written prayers of the Prayer Book in corporate worship. God is described as a friend (John 15:15) and he invites us to pray with the same familiarity as a son talking to his father ("When you pray, say, 'Our Father . . .'"). In private prayer and for praying in small groups the most natural form is usually spontaneous or extemporaneous prayer. But when we worship corporately we usually use a form and prayers from the Prayer Book. It's our way of guaranteeing that everything in worship is done "decently and in order" (1 Cor. 14:40). The first Book of Common Prayer was published in 1549 and the second in 1552. Thomas Cranmer, then Archbishop of Canterbury, authored both. Since then there have been other revisions, all of them based on the rule: periodic change is necessary and good as long as the revisions remain faithful to the teaching of Holy Scripture ("Preface" p. 10). Most Episcopalians and other Anglicans in America use the American Prayer Book revised in 1979, but some still prefer the 1928 Prayer Book.

Every church has rituals and structure, even the so-called "non-liturgi-cal churches." In fact they can be as structured about their non-structure as we are about our structure! Episcopal worship is based on several important affirmations. First, corporate Sunday worship is the most meaningful when worshippers have said their personal daily prayers between Sundays. One isn't a substitute for the other and both are necessary for Christian growth. Also, some Episcopalians find it helpful to come five or ten minutes early to church to quiet themselves and prepare their hearts to receive from God and worship him. Many also find it helpful to read the Bible lessons for the day before they come so that they are primed to hear God's Word.

Second, we frame our Sunday worship in the words that Christians throughout history have found helpful in expressing their concerns to God. This not only insures continuity to our theological tradition, it also keeps us from the kind of shallow individualism of prayers that are sometimes prayed from Protestant pulpits. Theologian and seminary dean Paul Zahl said,

> We use a book because the inherited wisdom of the past is often more trustworthy than the moods and opinions of the present moment. Yes, we desire our prayers to breath conviction and humility. But we would not wish our prayers to be formed by whatever is just passing through our heads.[51]

Prayer Book prayers are some of the most beautiful literary treasures in the English language and they are rich in theological content and meaning. They have stood the test of time. When we pray these prayers we pray in concert with those who have prayed them over the centuries (this is called "The Communion of Saints"). The Bible tells us that there will be much praising and worshipping going on in Heaven (Rev. 4,5). This means that when we worship, our prayers and praises join with those already in progress in heaven.

And lastly, Episcopalians affirm that worship is everyone's business, not just a minister on stage saying prayers for us. We see this especially in the responses that are invited from the congregation: "And also with you," "And blessed be his kingdom," "We lift them up to the Lord." The word "liturgy" literally means "the work of the people." The minister's job is not to entertain the troops or dazzle the crowds but to lead the congregation into the presence of the great and awesome God. It's every Christian's responsibility to contribute to worship by coming with prepared and expectant hearts, ready to give their voices and lives to God in singing and praying. When Christians make the prayers that the faithful have powerfully prayed over the centuries their own personal prayers, when the words of our songs truly express the singing in our hearts, and when we come with confidence that we will meet the Risen Lord, we experience what the Psalmist wrote: "In your presence there is fullness of joy; in your right hand are pleasures forevermore!" (Ps. 16:11).

Why is the service called "The Holy Eucharist?"

What Episcopalians call "The Eucharist" is called different things by different churches (the Divine Liturgy, the Lord's Supper, the Mass, etc.). "Eucharist" is the English equivalent of the Greek word for "thanksgiving," and it's the most ancient term for what we do. This one word encapsulates the essence of Christian worship: we offer God our profound thanks for his gift of salvation and for all his blessings.

There are two parts to the Holy Eucharist service: the Liturgy of the Word and Holy Communion — word and sacrament. History gives us a reason for this structure. The Bible tells us that the first Christians were Jews and when they first believed in Jesus as the Messiah there was no reason to stop the practice of attending synagogue worship on the Sabbath (Saturday). In addition, on the day of the Lord's resurrection (Sunday), they also met to observe the celebration of Holy Communion that Jesus commanded ("Do this in remembrance of me" 1 Cor. 11). These two observances continued roughly until the Romans destroyed Jerusalem in the year A.D. 70. Christians were then forced to leave Jerusalem, providing the occasion to bring into one Sunday worship experience the elements of the Saturday synagogue worship (i.e., the word) and the Sunday observance of Holy Communion (i.e., the sacrament).

The Liturgy of the Word is made up of the same elements of the

Jewish synagogue service: prayers, readings from Holy Scripture, a sermon, and an offering. And Holy Communion is the distinctly "Christian" part, using bread and wine to celebrate Jesus' real presence in our lives. Where some denominations focus mostly on the Word (many Protestant churches where the sermon is the focal point), and others on Holy Communion (Roman Catholics and Orthodox where the communion meal is often more important than the sermon), Episcopalians regard them both highly.

The two parts of our worship are bridged by what is called "The Peace" — when the congregation stands to greet one another with the words, "the peace of the Lord be with you." The Peace symbolizes our commitment to Christian love and forgiveness that is the foundation for Christian community. Jesus said that if you come to worship and there remember that someone has something against you, first go to be reconciled and then come back to make your offering (Matt. 5:23). At this point in the service, having obtained peace with God through confession of sins, we then proclaim and demonstrate our peace with one another. The Peace is a solemn prayer and blessing that we pray for one another. It is far more than a prelude to social hour or a way to get the kids in church from Sunday school. In the early church, new Christians studied for many months, sometimes years, before they could be baptized. In those days, people who were not yet baptized were dismissed with The Peace because only baptized Christians could participate in the Lord's Supper. Today Holy Communion is still reserved for Christians who wish to renew their relationship with Jesus Christ.

Episcopalians worship God in a variety of ways, from times of private prayer and praise to corporate Sunday worship, from informal Eucharists at church picnics to formal high celebrations at cathedrals. But each time we worship we want to be respectful of the amazing privilege it is to meet the King of kings and the Lord of lords!

DISCUSSION QUESTIONS

1. What are the distinguishing features of "Episcopal" worship?

2. Do you agree with the statement that there are no non-liturgical churches?

3. Why do Episcopalians "read" their prayers? What are the blessings and potential pitfalls of such a tradition?

4. How does someone make the words of the liturgy their personal prayers? How can you keep the "form" of worship alive, personal, and heart-felt?

5. Read what the Catechism says about corporate worship (p. 857). How well does your worship experience measure up to those objectives?

Chapter 8

Born again Episcopalians – an oxymoron?

If someone from another planet visited an Episcopal Church and observed a baptism or communion service, his journal entry might read:

How odd! Some kind of sadistic washing: parents smile dotingly while their baby suffers under cold water. And what looks like bread and wine is eaten, sometimes with tearful appreciation, by people who apparently think this is someone's body and blood! Strange people, those Episcopalians!

Strange as it might sound, Episcopalians believe that God works in and through the sacraments. The word "sacrament" comes from the Latin word meaning "pledge" – they come with God's pledge, his promise, to really work in our lives. They are more than symbols; they deliver the free and life-changing love of God ("effectual signs of Grace . . . towards us" Article XXV, p. 872). Sacraments are one of many ways that God works in the world today, but they **are** one way that God's grace connects with God's people. Theologian Donald Bloesch says that "sacraments announce that Jesus is present; faith receives and acclaims this presence; faith working through love demonstrates and manifests this presence to the world."[52]

We give the name "sacrament" primarily to Baptism and Holy Communion, "the two great sacraments given by Christ to his Church"

(p. 858). These hold preeminence over other sacramental rites[53] because Jesus personally commanded their observance ("go therefore and make disciples, baptizing . . . " and "do this [Holy Communion] in remembrance of me" (1 Cor. 11).

What does baptism do?

Baptism is called the "sacrament of new birth." Since baptism announces Jesus' presence, does this mean that becoming a Christian is the same thing as being baptized? Or does spiritual birth happen before, after, or quite apart from baptism? The experience of new birth, as it's described in the Bible, has two sides: God's gift and the receiving of the gift – what God does and what we do. Sacraments are primarily God acting toward us, not us towards him.[54] For the grace extended to us in baptism to be effective, it must be received by faith.[55] Believing God and entering the new life sometimes begins before and sometimes after baptism. Faith is not something we do to earn God's love; it is simply agreeing to be loved by our Heavenly Father and trusting him for salvation based on his completed work on the cross (cf. John 1:12; Rom. 10:9,13).[56] Theologian Michael Green says,

> Baptism is the pledge of God's new life. But it is like a seed: it only germinates when it encounters the water of repentance and sunshine of faith . . . Baptism puts you into Christ, if you let yourself be put.[57]

For example, someone could give you a wrapped present, but unless you open it and discover the gift inside you don't have a clue what its value is or any appreciation for its significance. It's a ridiculous thought, but someone could conceivably go through their whole life with the gift in their hands and never open it. This describes some who were baptized as infants but have never really entered the Kingdom of God that is prayed for in baptism and available to them by faith. Even though God's highest hope is for us to have eternal life, he will never force it on us or make us believe.

When someone is baptized in the name of the Father, Son, and Holy Spirit the church asks God to give them the abundant life (John 10:10). Specifically we pray for the forgiveness of sins (1 Pet. 3:21), that they will be joined with Christ in his death and resurrection (Rom. 6:3,4), for them to cross from this world into the kingdom of God (Col. 1:13,14), for spiritual birth (John 3:5), and that they will become a member of the church (1 Cor. 12:13). God actually gives these graces to the baptized, and, if they are met by faith, they become effective immediately. But if they are too young to understand or if they don't respond in faith, God's graces do not automatically effect what they symbolize.[58] As the Bible teaches, someone is not spiritually alive (i.e., born again) until he or she personally receives God's gift of salvation. Episcopalians have always believed that the grace given in the sacraments is effective in our lives only when it is met by personal faith – "They that receive Baptism rightly . . ." (Article XXVII, p. 873). "To all who received him, who believed in his name, he gave power to become children of God" (John 1:12).

Why not re-baptize?

Many Episcopalians and others who were baptized as infants have been lulled into thinking that baptism is enough. They have experienced the "outward sign" of baptism but haven't yet lived into the reality of their inheritance as God's children. They have been baptized but are not yet spiritually reborn. My favorite image for this is the man on an ox looking for an ox.[59] There he sits, heading off across the countryside looking for what is there the whole time. It's a pitiful picture, but it describes the life of everyone who fails to live into his or her baptism. The Apostle Paul describes something similar in his letter to the Ephesians: he told them that they were blessed in Christ with every spiritual blessing in the heavenly places (1:3). "Every blessing" obviously means that nothing was held back. So what's the problem in Ephesus? They simply didn't know how blessed they were. Paul went on to pray that the "eyes of their hearts would be enlightened so that they may know . . ." (vv. 17-19). It's totally possible to be blessed and not even know it – to have the outward sign without the inward grace. If you were baptized as a baby and now realize that you are not "born again" — and you want to be — the appropriate response is not to be "re-baptized." This would be an affront to the prayers that were prayed for you in baptism and an insult to God's goodness in already answering those prayers. The appropriate response would be, in an act of humble faith, to accept God's gifts and thank him for the inheritance that has been waiting for you from your baptism — to accept Jesus as your Lord and Savior, and begin the new life with Christ. Episcopalians see this as "living into our baptisms."

Why baptize infants?

Roman Catholics emphasize the objective reality of God's grace and treat baptism as always affecting the new birth that it symbolizes. Protestants generally emphasize the subjective response that's required to receive the gift of new life, and they treat baptism only as a symbol of the new life God gave them when they were converted. Episcopalians hold a middle ground between these views.[60] We believe that God objectively extends his grace in baptism, that it is far more than just a symbol. But to access the grace requires a personal response of faith.

So, if sacramental grace remains an unopened present until it's opened by faith, why not hold off on baptism until a person is old enough to make a personal decision for Christ? Episcopalians, of course, baptize adults who have made an informed decision to follow Jesus as Lord, but we also baptize babies when their parents are Christians and they come wanting their children to experience the fullest of God's blessings. We baptize babies for several reasons:

1. Becoming a Christian and the rite of baptism are two very different acts that are always separated by time. Baptism either precedes or follows the experience of conversion (i.e., repentance and personally accepting God's gift of salvation), but Christ commands us to do both. All the references to baptism in the Bible emphasize God acting towards us, not us toward him.

2. God loves children. Jesus accepted and blessed children too young to respond, and the Bible says that children don't need conversion to become like adults; rather, adults need conversion to become like children (Mark 10:13-16). The New Testament suggests that children were included among the families who were baptized together (Acts 2:39; 16:5, 32, 34), but this can't be proved one way or the other.

3. Circumcision, baptism's Old Testament antecedent, was performed on Jewish boys eight days old as a pledge and promise of Covenant blessings. This was obviously long before they could decide for themselves, yet circumcised babies were considered full members of the faith community. In the same way, baptism brings us into full membership in the New Covenant community (Col. 2:11.12).

4. From the earliest Christians until the Anabaptists questioned the practice of infant baptism in the 16th century – for the first 1,500 years of Christendom – it was the universal practice of the church to baptize infants.[61]

5. And last, and most important of all, infant baptism is the best example there is of God's unconditional love. It's the perfect picture of grace. Obviously, a three-month-old can't do anything to contribute to his or her salvation, much less accept Jesus as their Savior. But God gives them the gift of new life anyway. Before we loved him, he loved us (1 John 4:10). No one is saved because they deserve it or have earned it, but only because God freely gives it. Long before we knew God's love, he died on the cross for our sins. So why baptize infants? Because there's no reason to withhold from children the greatest gift of all, and to welcome them into the community of believers who will love them into loving Jesus.

Parents of small children receive and hold the baptismal promises in trust until their children are ready to assume responsibility for themselves.

For all the reasons cited, Holy Baptism is far more than a social event or "having your child done." What happens in baptism has eternal consequences; it rocks heaven and causes angels to sing! (Luke 15:10). For this reason, parents who bring their younger children for baptism should be willing to attend pre-baptism instruction and show by their commitment to worship every Sunday and be involved in the ministry that they are serious about bringing their child up in the faith and life of the church. They should also choose godparents (called "Sponsors" in the Prayer Book) for their love of Jesus Christ and their willingness to help teach their son or daughter to know and love the Lord.

The alien visitor might be shocked, but for Episcopalians, sacraments represent no less than the free gift of new life in Christ. They announce that God is present! In the next chapter we will take a look at another sacrament: that strange Christian eating ritual (and I'm not talking about church pot-lucks!).

DISCUSSION QUESTIONS

1. What is a "sacrament?" (See "The Sacraments" p. 857, Article XXV
    p. 872, Article "C" p. 878)

2. Why do you suppose Jesus was baptized? (See Matthew 3:13-17)

3. What is the relationship between Holy Baptism and New Birth?
    For babies?
    For adults?

4. What do you know (remember personally or know from stories) of
    your own baptism?

5. What does baptism "mean" in the light of the prayer "Thanksgiving
    over the Water"? (pp. 306-7)

6. In the baptism service, the congregation is invited to "renew our own
    baptismal covenant" (p. 303). What does this mean and how can you
    prepare yourself for the next baptism service at your church?

Chapter 9

Cannibalism and Episcopal etiquette

I see a lot of different things when I distribute Holy Communion. Besides the humorous experiences of dropping the bread in awkward places and navigating around ladies hats and young children, I regularly see tears of joy and relief. A Sunday doesn't go by that I don't see someone who is deeply moved. It's obvious that something powerful and wonderful often happens between God and his people when they receive Holy Communion.

The word "Communion" comes from "common union," which might suggest that Holy Communion would be a focus for Christian unity. In fact, disagreements about the meaning of the Lord's Supper have caused more debates in the church than almost anything else. When Jesus said, "This is my body . . . this is my blood," did he mean his actual flesh and blood? Or, was he speaking poetically like when he said, "I am the door" or "I am the good shepherd?" So, what is the meaning of this strange eating ritual and why is it so important to Episcopalians?

Holy Communion

"Sacraments announce that Jesus is present; faith receives and acclaims this presence . . . "[62] God's part in Holy Communion is to show up (real presence). Our part is to receive him and be refreshed in the Holy Spirit as we eat the bread and drink the wine. On the night before he died, Jesus took the ordinary bread and wine of the Passover meal and assigned to them new meaning:

> *"This is my body which is given for you. Do this in remembrance of me . . . this is the new covenant in my blood. Do this, as often as you drink it, in remembrance of me"* (1 Co. 11:24, 25).

He said two things: "this is my Body/Blood" and, "do this in remembrance of me." These two assertions correspond to the two different ways Holy Communion has been understood in history. Roman Catholics focus mostly on the first understanding. Thomas Aquinas, a 13th century theologian, developed an elaborate explanation for the "real presence of Christ" that has dominated Catholic theology. Transubstantiation, as it's called, is the teaching that the bread and wine of Communion become the actual body and blood of Christ even though it still appears to be bread and wine. And the sacrifice of Jesus on the cross, Aquinas believed, is relived on the altar every time Holy Communion is celebrated.[63] Not only does this theory explain how it happens, but also when and how. From an Episcopal perspective, transubstantiation leaves little to mystery, and it detracts from the biblical teaching that Jesus was sacrificed once for all (Heb. 9:28).

Many Protestants, on the other hand, focus on the "remembrance" part. They see Communion as a symbolic meal and the occasion to remember the events of the Last Supper and the Crucifixion. As Jews each year celebrate God's deliverance from Egypt (i.e., the Passover), so Jesus instituted Holy Communion to be a constant reminder that he delivered us from the bondage of sin by his sacrifice on the cross. Holy Communion, then, is the opportunity to renew a relationship with God who is spiritually present.

Episcopalians sometimes disagree with one another about the meaning of the Eucharist, but we generally represent the middle way between Catholics and Baptists. Like Catholics, we believe that God is really present in the communion meal. But, unlike Catholics, we don't attempt to explain how it happens, when it happens, and what form it takes. Like the Baptists, we see Holy Communion as a time to remember what Jesus did and an opportunity for spiritual renewal. But unlike the Baptists, we believe that it is far more than a memorial meal – that Jesus meant it when he said "This is my body . . . this is my blood."

The middle way held by Episcopalians between "Transubstantiation" and "memorial supper" is seen in the words of administration in the first three Prayer Books. When the priest distributed bread using the first Book of Common Prayer (1549) he said, "The body of our Lord Jesus Christ" – suggesting a real presence understanding. The words were changed for the 1552 revision to: "Take them in remembrance" – suggesting a memorial supper understanding. And, in the 1559/1662 revisions, the Prayer Books that became the standard for many years, both sentences (and both ideas) were brought together: "The body of our Lord Jesus Christ which was given for thee, preserve thy body and soul unto everlasting life; take and eat them in remembrance that Christ died for thee, and feed on him in thy heart by faith with thanksgiving." These are the words of administration that we use today in our current Prayer Book Holy Eucharist Rite 1 service (p. 338).

As with every sacrament, the grace of Holy Communion is effective when it is faithfully received – ". . . to such as rightly, worthily, and with faith, receive the same" (Article XXVIII, p. 873). We recognize the importance of feeding on him in our hearts "by faith with thanksgiving." Since receiving Holy Communion is about receiving God's very life, it's important to prepare ourselves for Holy Communion. Paul wrote, "Whoever, therefore, eats the bread or drinks the cup of the Lord in an unworthy manner will be answerable for the body and blood of the Lord" (1 Cor. 11:27). He goes on in the next verse to say, "Examine yourselves." "It is required that we should examine our lives, repent of our sins, and be in love and charity with all people" (p. 860). This doesn't mean that we have to be perfect to come to the Lord's Table, only that we are aware of our need and ready to receive his grace and mercy. Every Christian wishing to meet Jesus in the sacrament and be refreshed in his presence is welcome to receive Holy Communion.

The New Testament teaches us several things about Holy Communion:

First, coming to Communion is not an optional, take-it-or-leave-it experience for Christians. Jesus commanded his followers to "**do this** in remembrance of me." He never made such a command for Bible study, or prayer, or committee meetings. It is obviously a priority for Jesus that we continue this observance as a central feature of our corporate life.

Second, in Holy Communion we look forward to the day that Jesus will come again – when there will be a great heavenly banquet! "Truly I tell you," Jesus said at the Last Supper, "I will never again drink of the fruit of the vine until that day when I drink it new in the kingdom of God" (Mark 14:25). St. Paul likewise instructs us to continue to celebrate Holy Communion until Jesus comes back (1 Cor. 11:26). Communion is a foretaste of heaven in a day when few people give much thought to life after death or have much hope for heaven.[64] The most obvious reason the first Christians were so excited and joyful was because they really believed that Jesus was coming back any day. They were anxious to experience the final installment of the Kingdom of God. Our experience as Christians is either rote and anemic or alive and vibrant directly proportional to how much hope we have for heaven. Holy Communion proclaims that Jesus will one day come back to establish his kingdom forever: "Christ has died; Christ is risen; Christ **will** come again" (p. 363). It reminds us that Christ in us is "the hope of glory!" (Col. 1:27).

Third, Communion reminds us that the church is central to God's plan. "Because there is one bread, we who are many are one body, for we all partake of the one bread" (1 Cor. 10:17). We are born again, not in isolation, but into a Christian family. I laughed when I first saw the bumper sticker: Lord, save me from your followers. Anyone who has been ambushed by pushy Christians or victimized by vulgar evangelism can empathize with the saying. However, it falsely suggests that someone can be a growing and healthy Christian and not be in the church that Jesus

Christ started and heads. No church is perfect and there are hypocrites in every one of them. Maybe many! But the church is God's idea and his plan for growing Christians (Eph. 3:10). Holy Communion reminds us where we are nourished.

And lastly, and most wonderful of all, when we "feed on him in [our] hearts by faith" (p. 365) we feed on Jesus himself. He comes into us and dines with us (Rev. 3:20); he makes his home in us (John 14:23). As St. Paul said, "The cup of blessing that we bless, is it not a sharing in the blood of Christ? The bread that we break, is it not a sharing in the body of Christ?" (1 Cor. 10:16). Holy Communion is renewing the intimacy with Jesus that is our birthright as his children — to be "filled with thy grace and heavenly benediction, and made one body with him, that he may dwell in us and we in him" (p. 336).

A relatively recent change in the Episcopal Church is the practice of young children receiving Holy Communion. Before our most recent Prayer Book (1979), "Confirmation"[65] was considered the ticket for admittance to Communion. The sacrament was restricted to older children and adults. But in our current Prayer Book we've gone back to the more ancient understanding that baptism constitutes full membership. Even though it's left to the discretion of each family, with training from Christian parents, sponsors, and Sunday school programs, many are choosing to allow their young children to receive the sacrament. The most compelling reason for this is that, even though they obviously do not have an adult understanding of Holy Communion, even very young children have a growing understanding and appreciation for what is so central to our worship. Holy Communion is ultimately a mystery for children *and adults*, and no one really "knows enough" to earn the right to receive Communion.

The post-Communion prayers (pp. 365, 366) remind us that we are fed for a purpose. We are blessed to be a blessing to the world. In Holy Communion we are empowered for our most important ministry as

Christians: to be God's witnesses. Although the sacrament offers us much comfort, consolation, and healing, its final purpose is to make us strong for God in our families, neighborhoods, and workplaces. "And now, Father, send us out to do the work you have given us to do . . ."

In the next chapter of *Cranmer's Church* we will examine other means of receiving God's grace besides the sacraments.

DISCUSSION QUESTIONS

1. Some people in the first century, when they heard about Holy Communion, thought Christians practice cannibalism. How could they have this understanding, and what do Episcopalians believe? (See Article XXVIII, p. 873)

2. How do Roman Catholics differ from Baptists in their understanding of this sacrament?

3. Read and discuss "The Holy Eucharist" (p. 859). What did you learn that you didn't know before?

4. In what way is Christ present in the Communion service? What personal experiences have you had with God at the Communion Table?

5. Should young children be admitted to Holy Communion? Explain your answer.

6. What can you do this week to prepare yourself for the next time you will receive Holy Communion?

Chapter 10

Sign on the dotted line

O ne of my favorite cartoons shows a traditional-looking church with a sign in front that reads: "THE LITE CHURCH: 24% fewer commitments, home of the 7.5 tithe, 15-minute sermons, 45-minute Worship Services. We have only 8 Commandments — your choice. We use the 3 Spiritual Laws and have an 800-year millennium. **Everything you've wanted in a church . . . and less!**"

Is this what people want from church: one that asks for little and expects even less? Apparently some do. Some churches have grown huge on this basis. They cater to the consumer, one-stop-shopping, entertainment mentality that offers church-lite for those who are drawn to feel-good churchianity. But this doesn't describe the Episcopal Church. To be a member involves certain commitments and responsibilities.

Because baptism signifies full membership, the prayers we pray at baptisms (p. 305) will tell us much about the privileges and responsibilities of church membership. This is what we pray for and what is asked of church members:

DELIVER THEM, O LORD, FROM THE WAY OF SIN AND DEATH.
Every Episcopalian is expected to have an enjoyable and personal relationship with Jesus Christ.

This is the heart of the matter: not a religion or a life philosophy but a relationship with the living God. God delivers us with the same power that he delivered the Israelites from their bondage in Egypt, that he rescued

Jonah from the belly of the fish, and that he saved King David from debilitating guilt and depression. Sin is the last hurdle that keeps us from God, and death is the last enemy. To be delivered from sin is to be perfectly forgiven so that we can come to God unencumbered. To be delivered from spiritual death is to enter into everlasting life. Paul put it this way, "He has rescued us from the power of darkness and transferred us into the kingdom of his beloved Son" (Col. 1:13). It isn't enough to periodically attend church, occasionally pray (usually in the ancient and hallowed way: "help!"), and live relatively decent lives. It's possible to do all that and still miss a personal relationship with God. It's the difference between knowing someone second-hand from reading a book about him, and actually spending time with the person to get to know him. Although the prayer is written in the negative — "deliverance from" — the positive side is entrance into a new life and a new relationship. "When someone becomes a Christian, he becomes a brand new person inside. A new life has begun!" (2 Cor. 5:16, The Living Bible). When someone comes to Jesus for forgiveness and accepts him as Lord and Savior there are eternal ramifications: "there is rejoicing in heaven!" (Matt. 18:14).

OPEN THEIR HEARTS TO YOUR GRACE AND TRUTH.

Every Episcopalian is expected to have a daily time to meet with God for prayer and Bible reading.

A heart first cracks opens when someone meets God and accepts the gift of salvation. It opens more and more as we meet with him regularly. I don't know of a Christian anywhere who has a growing and exciting relationship with God who doesn't also have a daily practice of prayer, Bible reading, and personal worship. Spending time with God brings us into the neighborhood where his grace and truth live. There are lots of ways to have quiet times, and varying the routine from time to time can be very helpful. Most people find it helpful to have a regular time every day, in a quiet place, for a reasonable period (maybe beginning with 10-15 minutes a day). It's all based on the promise that if you "draw near to God, he will draw near to you" (James 4:8).

When you arrive for your appointment with God he will be waiting for you. You can never turn your attention to him and surprise him. Like the father in the Prodigal Son story (Luke 15), God is always waiting for you to come home. Some have found it helpful to include these four aspects of prayer:

*A*doration,
*C*onfession,
*T*hanksgiving, and
*S*upplication (or intercession)
(Remember: ACTS.)

Another way is to pray through the Lord's Prayer as a model prayer, taking time between each of the petitions to add your own personal prayers. There are also some good resources for individual and family prayers in the Prayer Book (e.g., p. 135).

After prayer, take time to read and reflect on a portion of Scripture. Before and after you read the Bible it helps to pray something like, "Lord Jesus, please open my mind and heart to your Word, and make me ready to obey it no matter how challenging or difficult." You might consider asking the following questions of the passage (*remember: SPECK*):
Is there

A *S*in to avoid?
A *P*romise to claim?
An *E*xample to follow?
A *C*ommand to obey?
How can this passage increase my *K*nowledge about God?

Some people also find it helpful to memorize scripture, sing hymns, and read spiritually uplifting books in their quiet times. The prayer for hearts open to grace and truth is answered when we meet God every day for prayer and study.

FILL THEM WITH YOUR HOLY AND LIFE-GIVING SPIRIT.

Every Episcopalian is expected to use their God-given gifts and abilities to help people in need.

God fills us with his Holy Spirit to empower us for ministry. Some churches teach that there are two classes of Christians: a minister who ministers and a congregation that congregates. But this betrays what the Bible teaches! In fact, every Christian is either a minister or they are denying God's highest call on their life. One day Jethro, Moses' father-in-law, observed Moses' workaholic tendencies. He was wearing out and the people he judged were wearing out, too (Exod. 18:13ff.). After pointing this out to Moses, Jethro encouraged him to "share the ministry." As he did, the Holy Spirit that was in him was divided among the new ministers (Num. 11:25), and Moses spoke of a time in the future when there will be a kingdom full of priests. His prophecy was fulfilled on the day of Pentecost when the Holy Spirit filled all the disciples and was made available to everyone (Acts 2:17). Peter wrote, "Like living stones, let yourselves be built into a spiritual house, to be a holy priesthood . . ." (1 Pet. 2:5). And Paul, writing in 1 Corinthians, said, "to each is given the manifestation of the Spirit for the common good" (12:7). The strength of any church is directly proportional to the number of God's people involved in ministry (See "Who are the ministers of the Church?" p. 855). If you are thinking that the Holy Spirit is given just to make you feel warm and fuzzy inside, you are missing the point. Every Episcopalian has a ministry through the empowering Holy Spirit, and each is expected to use their talents and abilities for God's service in the church and in the world.

KEEP THEM IN THE FAITH AND COMMUNION OF YOUR HOLY CHURCH.

Every Episcopalian is expected to worship every Sunday with their church family and to take advantage of the opportunities provided by the church to grow spiritually.

"Church" is God's idea and it's the instrument he chooses to grow his people. The Christian faith is a personal faith, but it's not a private faith. When we were "born again," we were born into a new family: God's family. And membership in this family is as important as membership in our biological families. The church is "holy" because its values are different and distinct from the unbelieving world. It's an oasis in the desert of warring passions. The church is a prelude and reflection of the fellowship we expect to enjoy in heaven. "The Church is holy, because the Holy Spirit dwells in it, consecrates its members, and guides them to do God's work" (p. 854). That's why it's so important to find a church that is firmly committed to biblical teaching and doctrine. These days, when commitments are few and shallow, some consider church attendance and involvement about as seriously as attending a service club – they go if there's not a better offer. The author of Hebrews warned against "neglecting to meet together, as is the habit of some . . ." (10:25). Keeping the Sabbath holy (the 4th Commandment), at the very least, involves worshipping every Sunday with your church family. If you have children, this means maintaining a family tradition that "going to church every Sunday is what this family does." This also means finding a church to attend when you are out of town or on vacation. "But," you say, "the church is full of hypocrites." Yes, but there's room for one more! "But," you say, "our current minister is not as good as the old one." Yes, but the church is about God and his people, not a particular minister. No church is without faults. I've heard it said that if you find a perfect church, don't join it, for then it will cease to be perfect. Christians who are growing in their love for God have a commitment to worship with their church family every week, and they take advantage of Sunday school classes, small groups, and other programs designed to grow strong Christians.

TEACH THEM TO LOVE OTHERS IN THE POWER OF THE SPIRIT.
Episcopalians are expected to be actively involved in a small, supportive group of Christian friends.

There's a world of difference between "going" to church and "being" the church for one another. One is building-oriented, the other focuses on relationships. As nice as some church buildings are and as helpful as they can be to support Christian community, we miss the point if we come and go to a geographical location but fail to know one another and invest our lives in one another. Unless a church is very small (a small group itself), it's important to view church as a network of small groups. Being a member of a small group, whether it's the church choir, a ministry team, or a home Bible study group, provides the opportunity for Christian friendships. This is where real Christian ministry and caring takes place. It's where Christians can be accountable to one another for their growth in Christ. No church buildings were constructed until about 300 years after Christ, but in those years Christianity exploded in size around the world because their focus was on building people, not buildings. Jesus' whole ministry was given to a small group of twelve disciples. Small groups were the main structure for the church for the New Testament Christians (Acts 2:46; 10:22; 12:12; 16:32; 20:7; 21:8). Christians who are growing in their love for God and in their love for one another know the wonderful blessing of being in a small group of Christian friends.

SEND THEM INTO THE WORLD IN WITNESS TO YOUR LOVE.
Every Episcopalian is expected to be ready and willing to share about the love of God as Christian witnesses.

How can we best serve God? By being nice? Raising good kids? Ushering at church? All of these are good, but our *primary* ministry is to "represent Christ and his Church; *to bear witness* to him wherever [we] may be . . ." (p. 855). Just before he ascended to heaven Jesus told the disciples to wait until they were empowered by the Holy Spirit, then "you will be *my witnesses* in Jerusalem, in all Judea and Samaria, and to the ends of the earth" (Acts 1:8). Every Sunday we end the Holy Eucharist service with the Prayer of Thanksgiving which is really a prayer for mission: "And now, Father, send us out to do the work you have given us to do, to love and serve you *as faithful witnesses* of Christ our Lord" (p. 366). A witness is someone who sees something and then tells others what they saw. Our highest calling is to witness to the love of God to everyone we meet – to live for God in our homes, neighborhoods and workplaces. A great way to do this is to invite a relative, friend or neighbor to come to church with you. There is nothing more winsome and magnetic than to see Christians interacting with God and with one another (John 17:21). But those who will never come to church on their own also need to see God in the lives of Christians. Repeated encounters with loving Christians is what prepares the way for our friends to come to know God personally.

Witnesses take the hope of the gospel into a hurting world. The church exists for reasons outside itself: for those who are not yet members. Every member of the Episcopal Church has a part to play. There's no greater blessing than helping introduce someone to God. And Christians earn the right to share the gospel when we prove our love for the world by offering practical help and support to those who are hurting. For this reason Episcopalians should fill all the boards and serve on the front lines of every agency whose purpose is to relieve suffering. Every member should consider going on a short-term or a long-term mission trip, or at least prayerfully and monetarily supporting others who go. After all, Jesus said that our "witness" should extend to the ends of the earth (Acts 1:8).

BRING THEM TO THE FULLNESS OF YOUR PEACE AND GLORY.
Membership in the Episcopal Church means having the habit of forgiveness, and a sense of joy and generosity.

We don't get the whole package all at once, but the more we walk with Christ, the more he will lead us to deeper lessons and to greater commitments. God wants us to grow and change so that we will better reflect his glory. For example, pretty soon into our new life we will learn the importance of forgiveness. Because we are human we sometimes do thoughtless things and hurt each another. Theologian Søren Kierkegaard said that Christians are like porcupines on a cold night; the colder it gets, the closer we get for warmth, and the closer we get, the more we poke and hurt one another. But keeping a grudge or nursing a hurt is not an option. The foundation for Christian community is the habit of forgiveness. Jesus said that his forgiveness of us is contingent on our willingness to forgive each other (Matt.6:14).

Joy is not necessarily the first thing that comes to your mind when you think of Episcopalians or their worship. A study of faces of those coming back from receiving Communion will sometimes show more duty and discipline than joy. But if joy is a fruit of the Spirit (Gal. 5:22), we should expect to grow in joy and especially our enjoyment of God. The Westminster Confession says that our chief objective is to know God and enjoy him forever. A joyless or boring Christian is worse than a boring unbeliever because we have every reason to be joyful and excited. The way to keep our relationship alive and exciting is to maintain a sense of the joy of the Lord. Nehemiah said, "The joy of the Lord is your strength" (8:10). Paul wrote, "For the kingdom of God is not food and drink but . . . joy in the Holy Spirit" (Rom. 14:17). A life lived from an enjoyable relationship with God and a commitment to share that joy with others is an adventurous life — "We are workers with you for your joy" wrote St. Paul to the Corinthians (2 Cor. 1:24).

Another area that touches on God's Lordship in our lives is the practice of Christian giving. In the beginning, it may seem like enough to throw a few dollars into the collection plate or write a token check. But you can't read the Bible for long before realizing that God directly links our spiritual life to money. In fact, the way we give is the best measure of how important God really is to us. Christian giving has nothing to do with the secular ideas of fundraising or paying our fair share. God doesn't need your money and the church will survive without your support. The truth is that we need to give — and to give generously and from the heart — because our spiritual health depends on it. We give in order to be more like Jesus, whose very nature led him to give everything — including his own life — for our sake. When we give freely and generously we let go of that which might otherwise possess us and keep us from our highest loyalty to God. Episcopalians are expected to give in proportion to how grateful they are for what God has given them. When we give we have the sense of investing in things that really matter (Matt. 6:19-21). The Bible teaches that everything we have and all that we are is a gift from God, and the way to express our gratitude for God's generosity is to return at least a tithe (10%) for his Body, the church. This is the beginning though, and most Christians will be led to give much more.

Episcopalians are expected to . . .
1. Have an enjoyable and personal relationship with Jesus Christ.
2. Have a daily Quiet Time for prayer, Bible study, and private worship.
3. Use your God-given gifts and abilities for ministry.
4. Worship with your church family every Sunday.
5. Be involved in a small, supportive group of Christian friends.
6. Be prepared to share God's love as Christian witnesses.
7. Maintain a habit of forgiveness, a sense of joy and generosity.

DISCUSSION QUESTIONS

1. How is your relationship with God?
   a. Warm and personal.
   b. Sometimes warm, sometimes cold.
   c. Cold most of the time.
   d. Never felt God's warmth.

2. What successes and failures have you had in trying to keep a daily Quiet Time of prayer and study? If you've never had this practice, is it something you might try?

3. Would you say that you have or have not discovered your spiritual gifts for Christian ministry? If "yes," what are they and how are you using them? If "no," how can you go about discovering them?

4. Do you know someone who is not a Christian? What can you do for him/her to "witness" to them the love of God?

5. Read Malachi 3:6-10. How were God's people disobedient?
   How could they return to the Lord?
   How does this lesson challenge your own practice of giving?

Postlude

Joy comes in the morning

On October 18, 2004, the sky fell on the Episcopal Church: the Windsor Report was released in London while the entire Anglican world waited with baited breath. Following the Windsor Report, the official response of the Eames Commission, Episcopal and Anglican leaders scurried to respond with a multitude of comments and pronouncements. Cranmer's Church would be changed forever as the Anglican community through the Windsor Report expressed the depth of the betrayal it felt towards the Episcopal Church. The immediate cause of the report was the decision of the 2003 General Convention to approve a non-celibate homosexual to be bishop of the Diocese of New Hampshire. This was done against the strongest urgings of the rest of the Communion, not to mention what the Bible teaches about human sexuality and 2,000 years of church history. The end result is that the Episcopal Church by action of General Convention chose to walk apart from the Anglican Communion.

How did we become so disconnected? In recent years, while the vast majority of the Communion held to the primary authority of the Bible and to the "substance of the faith," America's expression of Anglicanism raced off to new theologies revising itself right out of mainstream Christianity. While the rest of Anglicanism was committed to personal evangelism and to the strength of the local church, the Episcopal Church constructed big national and diocesan bureaucracies that increasingly separated the leaders from the people in the pews. While bishops around the world served the church as "defenders of the faith," Episcopal bishops have largely been unwilling to confront blatant heresy and false teaching in their own house. In short, the Episcopal Church has wandered away from Cranmer's Church, moved to another town, and assumed a whole new identity!

The Windsor Report gives biblical and traditional Episcopalians new hope for a structure that will link us to the healthy parts of the Anglican Communion. Hope for Cranmer's Church is not, as some think, in the four "instruments of unity" (described in the Windsor Report: the Archbishop of Canterbury, the Lambeth Conference, the Anglican Consultative Council, and the Primates' Meeting). These instruments are helpful for unity only inasmuch as they fulfill their function of upholding the historic teaching of the church. This is a new and exciting day for Cranmer's Church. Whatever the realignment will bring, whether or not we will be called Episcopalian or Anglican when the dust settles, and whether we look to Abuja Nigeria or New York City or London as the seat of Anglican authority, Cranmer's Church in America will assuredly continue on as a blessing to many as it has been for these many years.

"Weeping may last for the night, but joy comes in the morning!" (Ps. 30:5).

Appendix and Notes

APPENDIX 1

We believe in the . . . catholic church

Episcopalians are (small "c") catholic, as we affirm each Sunday when we recite the Nicene Creed. We are catholic in the traditional sense (not Roman Catholic): committed to the historic faith of the church that is also called the "ancient consensual faith" or "classical Christianity."[66]

Ignatius first used the word "catholic" in the second century A.D., but Vincent of Lerins, writing in the fifth century, articulated the clearest formation of the catholic principle in the ancient church:

> *In the catholic church itself, all possible care must be taken, that we hold **that faith which has been believed everywhere, always, by all**. For that is truly and in the strictest sense 'catholic,' which, as the name itself and the reason of the thing declared, comprehends all universality.*

Accordingly, the test of orthodoxy (right praise or right theology) is whether or not a particular teaching has the support of the theological consensus of historic Christianity. Another word for this is "tradition." Owen Chadwick writes, "A 'Catholic mind' is a Christian mind with a sense of Christian history."[67] Anglican theologian Richard Hooker, always honoring the primary authority of Scripture, thought of tradition as the church's interpretation of Scripture over time. The New Testament says that there is a body of unchanging truth passed on to each generation that will connect us to the teaching of the apostles. Jude spoke of this as "the faith that was once and for all entrusted to the saints" (3); Paul called it "the common faith" (Titus 1:4) and "the faith of the gospel" (Phil. 1:27). The Prayer Book calls it "the substance of the faith" (p. 9).

This means, first, that the church is universal: that what is true is true for all people at all times. Revealed truth travels in a space above time, culture, or how I feel on any particular day. The Catechism says: "The Church is catholic, because it proclaims the whole Faith to all people, to the end of time" (p. 854).

Secondly, each generation is connected to the one before and the one that follows it by the common faith of the church. This passing on of the teachings of Scripture is called Apostolic Succession. Because bishops are "defenders of the faith," Apostolic Succession is symbolized by the laying on of hands when bishops consecrate new bishops. It's important for the church to change from time to time to accommodate the changes in culture. Worship styles change, for example, and need to be updated in each generation. But our core theology, which includes Scripture teaching on morals, never changes. It remains relevant and life-giving for each generation. Theologian Thomas Oden said, "Teaching tested by many generations is stronger than teaching checked out by only one generation."[68] This is what it means to be catholic Christians.

Each time we say, "We believe in one holy **catholic** and apostolic church" we restate our commitment to the authority of the Bible as interpreted over time. The faith once and for all entrusted to the saints is the rock on which Episcopalian theology is built. This powerful affirmation causes a lot of wild-eyed bishops and clergy to stutter and slur their speech at least once a week precisely at this point in the service. You can't be catholic in your faith and not know that the church has spoken decisively about the uniqueness of Jesus Christ, the doctrine of the Trinity, and about matters of human sexuality.

APPENDIX 2

Episcopalians and the Holy Spirit

When do we get the Holy Spirit? At baptism? When we commit our life to Christ? As a second blessing after conversion? John the Baptist is quoted in all four gospels as saying that Jesus, when he comes, will "baptize with the Holy Spirit." The image of baptism conjures up a picture of someone so intimately connected with the third person of the Trinity, whose every fiber of being is saturated with God's power, they are fully alive to the reality of God and equipped with every spiritual gift they need for ministry. Generally speaking, there are three views: the Catholic, the Evangelical, and the Charismatic or Pentecostal.

Catholics sees Baptism with the Holy Spirit as synonymous with water baptism. Paul wrote, "by the one spirit we were all baptized into one body," and, "we were all made to drink of one Spirit" [not two] (1 Cor. 12:13; Eph. 4:5).

Evangelicals believe that we receive the Spirit's baptism when we accept Jesus as Lord and Savior. After Peter's sermon on the Day of Pentecost, someone in the crowd asked, "What shall we do?" Peter answered, "Repent, and be baptized . . . and you shall receive the gift of the Holy Spirit" (2:38). Evangelicals argue that baptism is a sign of what has already happened (i.e., coming to Christ and receiving the Holy Spirit). They cite

Paul, "No one can say 'Jesus is Lord' except by the Holy Spirit" (1 Cor. 12:3), and "Anyone who does not have the Spirit of Christ does not belong to him" (Rom. 8:9).

Charismatics or *Pentecostals* see conversion as an initial installment of the Holy Spirit and the Baptism of the Holy Spirit as a second blessing – i.e., God's empowerment or the release of the Holy Spirit. They point out that on the first Easter night Jesus breathed on the disciples and said, "Receive the Holy Spirit" (John 20:22). Then, forty days later, just before he ascended, Jesus instructed the disciples not to leave Jerusalem, where "you will be baptized with the Holy Spirit not many days from now" (Acts 1:5). Ten days later, on the Feast of Pentecost, they are filled [again?] with the Holy Spirit (Acts 2:4). The usual expectation is that this subsequent baptism will be accompanied by speaking in tongues, the experience of those who were baptized with the Holy Spirit in the book of Acts.

Catholics appropriately emphasize that the Holy Spirit is a free, objective gift – God loved us before we loved him. Evangelicals are surely correct in connecting the experience of the Baptism of the Holy Spirit with its faithful reception, whether we receive the Spirit in baptism or when we accept Jesus as our Lord and Savior and live into our baptism. And Charismatics are certainly right in assuming that the Spirit's baptism is often an experience apart from baptism or conversion; that we should be filled and filled again with the Spirit throughout our Christian lives (Eph. 5:18).

As much as we would like to nail the Holy Spirit down, it's impossible. The Spirit comes and goes like the wind wherever he chooses (John 3:8). In some references it seems like the Spirit's baptism is the same as becoming a Christian. In other references it seems pretty clear that it is a separate experience of empowerment and anointing for ministry. None of the views does full justice to the Holy Spirit. The issue then is not WHEN or HOW you got the Holy Spirit, but that he fills your life today. It's not so much a question of, "How much of the Holy Spirit do you have?" as "How much of you does he have?" How yielded are you to the power of the Holy Spirit working in you and through you? Jesus said, "If you then, who are evil, know how to give good gifts to your children, how much more will the heavenly Father give the Holy Spirit to those who ask him!" (Luke 11:13). Why not ask God to fill you with his holy and life-giving Spirit?

Terry Fullam[69] first introduced me to eagles as a metaphor for the Spirit-filled life. Then one day I flew in a glider airplane above the Rocky Mountains and saw eagles for myself. Eagles are not like other birds. A chicken, for example, to get from one side of a pen to the other, feverishly flaps its wings to make it happen. But an eagle climbs to the edge of the cliff and waits. She waits, sometimes for long periods, until the wind comes along. When she feels the wind she opens her wings and the wind picks her up and carries her. Eagles don't fly like other birds; they soar. There are only two ways to live: in our own strength and wisdom and ingenuity, or in the power and wisdom of the Spirit who fills our lives. Long before Jesus, the prophet understood this when he wrote, "Those who wait for the Lord shall renew their strength, they shall mount up with wings like eagles, they shall run and not be weary, they shall walk and not faint" (Isa. 40:31).

APPENDIX 3

SOME EVENTS IMPORTANT TO "CRANMER'S CHURCH"

A.D. 33   Jesus: "Go into all the world to make disciples" Matt. 28.

Late 2nd cent.   Christians are now in Britain; perhaps Roman soldiers were the first missionaries on English soil.

3rd cent.   St. Alban. Britain's first Christian martyr.

314   Council of Arles. Three English bishops attend, suggesting well organized ecclesiastical structure.

596   Pope Gregory of Rome sends Augustine.

664   Council of Whitby. Roman Catholicism adopted officially. Before that, English Celtic form of Christianity.

1215   Magna Carta limited the power of English monarchs and guaranteed that the English Church would be free.

1384   John Wycliff, professor at Oxford, translates the Bible into English and calls for the church to return to the Bible and early church fathers (England's first Protestant).

14th, 15th cent.   Renaissance: revival in learning, art, and literature.

16th cent.   Undermined papal authority, making the Reformation inevitable.

1450	Gutenberg Bible. First moveable type printing, making Christian literature more widely available.

1517   95 Theses posted on Wittenberg door. Martin Luther initiates the Reformation in Germany. Luther's writings especially influencing scholars at Cambridge (White Horse Tavern).

1526   William Tyndale translates Bible into English straight from the Greek and Hebrew.

1534   King Henry VIII, the Act of Supremacy establishing the Church of England separate from Rome. Thomas Cranmer, then Archbishop of Canterbury, authorized the English Bible.

1539   Six Articles. Although Henry breaks with Rome, retains same religious practices: Transubstantiation, communion in one kind, permanent monastic vows, indulgences, auricular confession to priest, celibacy for clergy.

1549   First Book of Common Prayer and major reforms under "the boy king" Edward VI. Cranmer leads Anglicanism more fully into Protestantism. Mass becomes Communion meal; communion in 2 kinds; altar becomes table; Transubstantiation eliminated; prayers for the dead and references to purgatory eliminated; priests permitted to marry.

1553   Queen Mary seeks to re-Romanize. Cranmer, Ridley, Latimer, Hooper burned at stake.

1558	The Elizabethan Settlement. Queen Elizabeth I in her 45-year reign brings a broad comprehensiveness, fully Protestant but with the parts of Catholic heritage that can be supported by Holy Scripture.
1607	Jamestown, Virginia. Celebration of Lord's Supper in thanksgiving for safe arrival, John Smith and party of 104 colonists. But no Anglican bishops for another 177 years, until Seabury.
1640	Great Rebellion. Puritans in England, led by Cromwell, do away with monarchy, and the possibility of Anglican bishops in the colonies. Anglicanism suppressed.
1660	Charles II restores the church.
1730's to 1750's	Great Awakening. Spiritual revival led by George Whitfield and John Wesley (Methodist fame). Swept Great Britain as well as colonial America.
1776	American Revolution. Cuts off church from England.
1784	Samuel Seabury. Connecticut clergy choose Seabury to be first American bishop. Consecrated in Aberdeen, Scotland, bringing with him the demands of the Scottish Church.
1785	First General Convention in Philadelphia. The Protestant Episcopal Church becomes the first independent branch of Anglicanism.
1787	William White and Samuel Provost consecrated bishops at Lambeth Palace. Promise that American Episcopal Church will not alter doctrines of the Church of England.

1789	Prayer Book and Constitution and Canons adopted.
1801	Authority of "Thirty-Nine Articles" endorsed as the theological standard for the Episcopal Church.
1873	The Reformed Episcopal Church. Breakaway church, led by Evangelical assistant bishop of Kentucky George Cummins.
1800 to 1850	Moralizing influence of Evangelicals in England. William Wilberforce leads fight to abolish slavery 1830.
1830s	Oxford Movement. Seeks to return the church to pre-Reformation times.
1888	Chicago-Lambeth Quadrilateral. Bedrock essentials of Anglicanism. Bible is the ultimate standard of faith, the two creeds are sufficient statements of Christian faith, the two great sacraments are baptism and Holy Communion, and the historic place of bishops in the church.
1919	A National Council of the Episcopal Church is organized to carry out the functions of the General Convention between triennial meetings and office of the Presiding Bishop.
1928	3rd Book of Common Prayer (1st 1789, 2nd 1892).
1960	Dennis Bennett's Nine O'clock in the Morning. Episcopalians rediscover the power of the Holy Spirit.
1976	Trinity Episcopal School for Ministry founded in Ambridge, PA, to train clergy for ministry in the Anglican

Evangelical tradition. Same year, the ordination of the first women priests.

1979   Book of Common Prayer (our current version).

1991   George Carey elevated to Archbishop of Canterbury.

2002   Rowan Williams elevated to Archbishop of Canterbury.

2003   General Convention and consent to ordain Gene Robinson bishop of New Hampshire, the first openly gay bishop: the beginning of the realignment of the Anglican Communion and the Episcopal Church.

2004   The Windsor Report is delivered, mapping a strategy for the reordering of the Anglican Communion.

Notes

1. Called "the great and gifted compiler" and noted for "his love for synthesis," S. Leuenberger, *Archbishop Cranmer's Immortal Bequest* (Grand Rapids: Eerdmans, 1990) pp.183, 6.

2. P. Collinson, "Thomas Cranmer," *The English Religious Tradition and the Genius of Anglicanism*, ed. G. Rowell (Abingdon: Nashville, 1992), p. 87.

3. Reportedly "plain" by everyone else's standards.

4. See Appendix 1 "I believe in the catholic church . . ." p. 83.

5. A. Hudson, "John Wyclif," *The English Religious Tradition and the Genius of Anglicanism*, ed. G. Rowell, p. 76.

6. "By the time that Cranmer reached [Henry] in the small hours of that morning, Henry was already incapable of speech, but reached out to his old friend. 'Then the archbishop, exhorted him to put his trust in Christ, and to call upon his mercy, desired him, though he could not speak, yet to give some token with his eyes or with his hand, that he trusted in the Lord. The king, holding him with his hand, did wring his hand in his as hard as he could.' Quickly playing out his calling as royal chaplain, Cranmer had won a final victory in his years of argument with the King on justification. No last rites for Henry; no extreme unction; just an evangelical statement of faith in a grip of the hand." D. MacCulloch, *Thomas Cranmer: A Life* (New Haven: Yale Press, 1996), p. 360.

7. Many Episcopalians are more comfortable describing the Bible as the **supreme** authority (*suprema scriptura*) rather than the **only** authority (*sola scriptura*).

"There may be hallowed traditions, but no tradition is so hallowed as not to be up for question in each generation. We are encouraged to have a positive high doctrine of tradition – but the doctrine of Scripture *must* be higher; and that is the thrust of the Reformation formularies." C. Buchanan, *Is the Church of England Biblical? An Anglican Ecclesiology* (London: Darton Longman Todd, 1998), p. 197.

8.   J. C. Ryle, *Five English Reformers* (Carlisle PA, Banner of Truth Trust, 1981), p. 22.

9.   The term "Anglican" in reference to Elizabeth is, strictly speaking, anachronistic. Anglicanism, as a reference to a distinct theological position, was invented by John Henry Newman and first used in 1838. Soon thereafter it acquired the sense that we use today, of "pertaining to the Church of England." Sykes and Booty (ed.), "Anglicanism" J.R. Wright, *The Study of Anglicanism* (Minneapolis: Fortress, 1988), p. 424.

10.   "Elizabeth was theologically stunted, bound to a more or less 'confirmation class' level of Christian reflection . . . Elizabeth's 'Anglicanism' was and is a wax nose. It can be shaped in a Protestant direction, and it can be shaped in a Catholic or non-Roman but 'high church' direction. It can even be shaped in a 'liberal' or 'broad church' direction." P. Zahl "The Bishop-led Church," *Perspectives on Church Government*, ed. C.O. Brand and R.S. Norman (Broadman & Holman, Nashville, 2004), p. 222.

11.   R. Prichard, *A History of the Episcopal Church* (Harrisburg: Morehouse, 1991), p. 2.

12.   Today there are 38 semi-autonomous Provinces in the Anglican Communion, of which the Episcopal Church is one. According to the Windsor Report (see p. 80), the Anglican Communion is held together by a common heritage that is protected by certain instruments of unity.

13.   In recent years there has been some effort to change the name from "The Protestant Episcopal Church in the United States of America" (PECUSA) to "The Episcopal Church in the United States of America" (ECUSA). It seems that main-

taining the Bible as our primary authority, the hallmark of Protestantism, is an uncomfortable thought for some progressives. According to our current Constitution and Canons, however, our name is: The Protestant Episcopal Church in the United States of America, otherwise known as the Episcopal Church.

14.   C. Loveland, *The Critical Years: The Reconstitution of the Anglican Church in the United States of America: 1780-1789* (Seabury: CT, 1956), p. 61.

15.   Other "irregular" consecrations have occurred in modern times with the consecration of bishops for the Anglican Mission in America (AMiA) by African and Asian bishops in 2000. "Irregular" yes, but not without historic precedent.

16.   Cf. Loveland, p. 284. Also, David Summer, author of *The Episcopal Church's History 1945-1985*, wrote, "Like most church leaders, I believed that the diocese was the primary unity of the Episcopal Church, and that its strength – compared with those 'congregationalist churches' – was that we 'did things together.' . . . I've changed my mind. The diocese may be a structural convenience or necessity, but the local congregation is the most basic place where ministry takes place, hearts are healed, and lives are transformed. The diocese exists to enable the ministry of the local congregation and not the other way around." "It's the Congregation – Not the Diocese", *The Living Church* (June 9, 2002), p. 25.

17.   When two people sit down to a game of chess, they can do so only because they assume certain rules for their game. The Episcopal Church seems in danger of losing the sense of a common agreement about the rules. Until recent times there was at least basic agreement within the various schools of Episcopalian thought about the authority of Holy Scripture. Replacing the old standard today is a new religion of "personal experience" and "what feels right." Traditional Episcopalians and progressive Episcopalians are playing two different games and wishing the other would play by their rules!

18.   "Before 1820, Evangelical Episcopalianism was little more than a loose network of like-minded persons. By 1830, the clergy had succeeded in turning this network into a church party complete with its own defined theology, periodicals,

influential parishes, well-known leaders, and a theological seminary." D. Butler, *Standing Against the Whirlwind: Evangelical Episcopalians in Nineteenth-Century America* (Oxford: NY, 1995), p. 50.

19.   This is the subject of the last Tract: John Henry Newman's infamous Tract 90 (1841). Church historian Gillis Harp wrote an excellent critique of the various interpretations of the Thirty-Nine Articles in which he argues for a fair interpretation from the perspective of the "original intent of its framers." He wrote that "When the Anglican formularies become a kind of wax nose that can be shaped by partisans who were avowed enemies of the principles of the English Reformers, then is it any wonder that Anglicanism is in dire straits?" "Recovering Confessional Anglicanism," 2002 English journal *Churchman*, p. 235.

20.   Charles Gore, ed., *Lux mundi: a Series of Studies in the Religion of the Incarnation*, 10th edn. London: John Murray, 1890.

21.   Cf. Article VII, p. 869.

22.   G. Harp, *Brahmin Prophet: Phillips Brooks and the Path of Liberal Protestantism* (Rowman & Littlefield, NY, 2003), p. 138.

23.   Packer, Ware, Kreeft (ed.), P. Kreeft "Ecumenical Jihad," *Reclaiming the Great Tradition: Evangelicals, Catholics and Orthodox in Dialogue* (Downers Grove: InterVarsity, 1997), p. 23.

24.   "Reason is the basic human faculty of thinking, based on argument and evidence. It is theologically neutral, and poses no threat to faith — unless it is regarded as the only source of knowledge about God. It then becomes *rationalism*, which is an exclusive reliance upon human reason alone, and a refusal to allow any weight to be given to divine revelation." A. McGrath, *A Passion for Truth* (Downers Grove, IL: InterVarsity Press, 1996), p. 90,91.

25.   R.H. Fuller, "Scripture," *The Study of Anglicanism*, ed. Sykes and Booty, (Minneapolis: Fortress, 1988), p. 83.

26. D. MacCulloch, "The Myth of the English Reformation," The History Channel website.

27. "What Scripture doth plainly deliver, to that first place both of credit and obedience is due; the next whereunto is whatsoever any man can necessarily conclude by force of reason; after these the voice of the Church succeedeth. That which the Church by her ecclesiastical authority shall probably think and define to be true or good, must in congruity of reason over-rule all other inferior judgments whatsoever" (*Laws*, Book V, 8:2, Folger Edition 2:39, 8-14).

28. "A Stool or a Tower?" *The Anglican Digest* (Transfiguration 2005, Vol. 47, no.4), p. 11.

29. Seminary professor Michael Floyd exposes the *lex orandi* formula as a foreign idea to Anglicanism, and the three-legged stool as a "recent innovation, giving expression more to twentieth century ideas than to traditionally Anglican ones." "Are the Scriptures Still Sufficient?" *Our Heritage and Common Life*, ed. W. Adams and M. Floyd (University Press of America: Lanham MD, 1994), p 49.

30. Clergy in the Church of England are required to acknowledge The Articles as one of the historic documents of the church "which bear witness to the faith revealed in Scripture and set forth in the catholic creeds" (Canon C 15). Our first Presiding Bishop, William White, championed The Articles for the Episcopal Church; however, he did not feel that formal subscription to them was necessary since they were already included in the Constitution of the Church, and everyone ordained vowed to uphold the doctrine and discipline of the Church (including the Constitution).

31. Church historian Geoffrey Bromiley laments the fact that the Articles have been relegated to the basement of the Prayer Book (hidden in the historical documents section). "The current neglect or evasion or even defiance of The Articles is one of the greatest tragedies of modern Anglicanism." Quoted in "The Articles of Religion: Buried Alive?" by The Rev. Sam Pascoe (SEAD occasional paper No. 1, Nov. 1994).

32. "It doesn't occur to many people that what they call 'tolerance' is really sheer lack of conviction. It is not particularly significant if a man who has no great convictions says he is tolerant. Indeed, tolerance is a virtue only if a man believes something very strongly, yet respects the rights of others to disagree." L. Ford, *The Christian Persuader* (Minneapolis: World Wide Publications, 1988), p. 18.

33. "Generosity without orthodoxy is nothing, but orthodoxy without generosity is worse than nothing." Hans Frei quoted in B. McLaren, *A Generous Orthodoxy* (Grand Rapids: Zondervan, 2004), p.14.

34. I am forever indebted to J. Sidlow Baxter, *The Master Theme of the Bible* (Wheaton IL: Tyndale, 1973); P.T. Forsyth, *The Cruciality of the Cross* (Eugene OR: Wipf & Stock, 1997); and John R. W. Stott, *The Cross of Christ* (Downers Grove IL: InterVarsity Press, 1986).

35. The first hints of this are seen early in Genesis when God shed blood to cover Adam and Eve's sin and shame (3:21). Then, of the two offerings, Cain's and Abel's, the one that God accepted was the one that involved the shedding of blood (Gen. 4:4). A little later God himself provided the lamb for sacrifice (Gen. 22:8). The sacrifice that was acceptable to God involved the shedding of lambs blood for salvation and victory over death (Exod. 12:13). It required a spotless victim without blemish (Lev. 22:19-21). In Isaiah, the Prophet spoke for the first time about the sacrificial lamb as a person who would be born to die (53:7). Finally, the mystery of the ages and the hope of all humanity was revealed on the day that John the Baptist pointed down the road to Jesus and said, "Behold the Lamb of God that takes away the sins of the world" (John 1:36). Peter summed up the master theme of the Bible when he said that we were ransomed "with the precious blood of Christ, like that of a lamb without blemish or spot" (1 Pet. 1:19). John's vision of heaven spotlighted "a Lamb standing as though it had been slain" (Rev. 5:9; 21:22).

36. Cf. John 3:16. "When we set the two side by side – our heavy, weighty, monumental sin on one side of the balance, and the depth of God's love on the other side – the side of the scale holding love pounds resolutely on the foundations of the world and resounds throughout all ages." M. R. McMinn, *Why Sin Matters* (Wheaton: Tyndale, 2004), p. 17

37. We compromise the Bible's high Christology and low anthropology when we see ourselves as capable of addressing sin. "The lower we are made to go in knowing ourselves as sinners, the higher shall we rise in joy when assurance of God's pardon breaks in. To play down the sinfulness of sin is to obscure the greatness of grace." J. I. Packer quoted in S. Leuenberger, p. 276.

38. If you have prayed this prayer for the first time, you have made the most important decision of your life! Welcome into God's family. The Bible says that your decision has eternal consequences — angels are rejoicing in heaven (Luke 15:7)! Please make sure to share this with your minister or a strong Christian friend. They will want to encourage you and support you in your new life with Christ. Read the Gospel of John and marvel at God's extravagant love for you.

39. I personally heard Bishop John Spong give this talk at Rollins College in Winter Park, Florida, in the late 1980s.

40. L. Newbigin, *The Gospel in a Pluralistic Society* (Grand Rapids: Eerdmans, 1989), p. 21.

41. E.g., Romans 1:18-23; 1 Cor.10:20; 2 Thess. 2:9-12; 1 Tim. 4:1.

42. In addition, the seven "I am" sayings in John's gospel clearly identify Jesus with the God of the Bible who stated that his name is "I am" in Exodus 3:14. Cf. John 6:35; 8:12; 10:7; 10:11; 11:25; 14:6; 15:1. "Jesus said to them, 'Very truly, I tell you, before Abraham was, I am" (John 8:58).

43. "The Scope of the Cosmic Christ," *Grace and Truth in the Secular Age*, ed. Bradshaw (Grand Rapids: Eerdmans, 1998), p. 8.

44. *More Than One Way? Four Views on Salvation in a Pluralistic World* (Grand Rapids: Zondervan, 1995), p. 177.

45. *The Great Divorce* (New York: Macmillan Publishing, 1978), p. 72.

46. Attributed to D. T. Niles.

47. Newbigin, p. 72.

48. Cf. *Can A Bishop Be Wrong?* Ed. P. C. Moore (Harrisburg: Morehouse, 1998).

49. A diocese is a group of churches headed by a bishop. General Convention is a gathering of bishops and elected representatives from every diocese of the Episcopal Church that meets every three years (usually in a luxury hotel to pass resolutions on how we should be more compassionate toward those who could never afford to stay in such a nice hotel).

50. *The Rebirth of Orthodoxy* (San Francisco: Harper Collins, 2003), p. 31.

51. *The Beacon*, Fall 1999, Trinity Episcopal School for Ministry.

52. *The Church: Sacraments, Worship, Ministry, Mission* (Downers Grove, IL: InterVarsity Press, 2002), p. 175.

53. I.e., Confirmation, ordination, matrimony, confession, and anointing the sick with oil, p. 860.

54. "Cranmer knew that sacraments were God's ways of working, not man's; that the only appropriate human response was one of reception, with the organ of faith, itself a gift of God." P. Collinson, "Thomas Cranmer," p.95.

55. "The spiritual efficacy of these Ordinances is always conditional and is not to be associated in any absolute way with the simple administration and application of them. They have no spiritual power of themselves apart from the Spirit of God on God's side and faith on our side." G. H. Thomas, *The Catholic Faith* (London: Church Book Room Press, 1955), p. 103.

56. Any mother knows that life really begins before her child is actually born. The experience of new birth may be gradual or a sudden, bolt-of-lightning experience, but Episcopalians tend to focus more on the process than identifying an exact date and time.

57. *Baptism: Its Purpose, Practice and Power* (Downers Grove IL: InterVarsity, 1987), p. 56-57.

58. A famous ecclesiastical trial in 1850 addressed the question of whether or not a person is reborn automatically (*ex opere operato*) in Holy Baptism. Henry Philpotts, the Anglican Bishop of Exeter, refused to institute George Gorham as rector because he didn't believe that every baptized person was born again. Gorham won his case, and the Privy Council stated, "Grace may be granted before, in or after baptism . . . but only in such as worthily receive it." M. Green, Ibid., p. 57.

59. John Claypool, *The Preaching Event: Lyman Beecher Lectures* (Waco, TX: Word, 1980). p. 78.

60. Some interpret the words of the baptism service as endorsing a Catholic view: that a person is automatically reborn regardless of whether or not there is a faith response (see "Thanksgiving over the Water" p. 306). But as Bishop J. C. Ryle tells us, "The principle of the Prayer-book is to suppose all members of the Church to be in *reality* what they are in profession,- to be true believers in Christ . . . The Prayer-book takes the highest standard of what a Christian ought to be, and is all through worded accordingly . . . It supposes those who bring their children to be baptized bring them as *believers* . . . [but] in all cases *worthy reception* is essential to the full efficacy of the sacrament." *Knots Untied* (Cambridge: James Clarke, 1977), p.108.

61. The one interesting exception among the church fathers was Tertullian (A.D. 160-220) who objected to infant baptism, not on the grounds related to faithful reception, but because it "imposes too great a responsibility on the godparents; they might die and so be unable to fulfill their obligations", M. Green, p. 74.

62. Bloesch, p. 175.

63. For the entire history of Anglicanism [since the 1552 Prayer Book until the current 1979 Prayer Book] "altars" were deliberately referred to as "Holy Tables" or "the Lord's Table." The word "altar" was avoided because it suggests sacrifice

or re-sacrifices, and Episcopalians have never had this understanding of Holy Communion. By changing this in 1979 we have taken a step back into a pre-Reformation view of the sacraments that is foreign to historic Anglicanism. Also reinforcing this false view are the words of the fracture that are also new to the 1979 Prayer Book: "Christ our Passover is sacrificed for us" — rather than "was sacrificed" or "has been sacrificed" 1 Cor. 5:7.

64.   Jeremy Taylor, speaking of the blessing of Holy Communion, said that "nothing else but the actual enjoying of heaven is above it." quoted by K. Stevenson, *The Mystery of Baptism in the Anglican Tradition* (Harrisburg: Morehouse, 1998), p. 171.

65. "Confirmation" is the rite of the Episcopal Church for commissioning a person for a life of Spirit-filled ministry. It is when a person publicly assumes one's role as a responsible Christian. "Confirmation is the rite in which we express a mature commitment to Christ, and receive strength from the Holy Spirit through prayer and the laying on of hands by a bishop" (p. 860).

66.   Oden, p. 31.

67.   Chadwick, p. 308.

68.   Oden, p. 125.

69. The one-time rector of St. Paul's Episcopal Church, Darien, CT, and the author of several books.